YOU CAN

Improve
your children's
WRITING

Celia Warren

FOR AGES
7-11

"...pupils continue to find it difficult to produce their best writing unaided.."
DfES

Author

Celia Warren

Editor

Sally Gray

Development Editor

Kate Pedlar

Series Designer

Joy Monkhouse

Cover designer

Anna Oliwa

Cover illustration

© Design pics inc/alamy.com

Design and Illustrations

Q2a Media

Text © Celia Warren

© 2007 Scholastic Ltd

Designed using Adobe InDesign

Published by Scholastic Ltd
Villiers House
Clarendon Avenue
Leamington Spa
Warwickshire CV32 5PR

www.scholastic.co.uk

Printed by Bell and Bain Ltd.
1 2 3 4 5 6 7 8 9   7 8 9 0 1 2 3 4

British Library Cataloguing-in-Publication Data
A catalogue record for this book is available from the British Library.
ISBN 0-439-945-318
ISBN 978-0439-94531-8

The right of Celia Warren to be identified as the author of this work has been asserted by her in accordance with the Copyright, Designs and Patents Act 1988.

Extracts from The National Literacy Strategy © Crown copyright. Reproduced under the terms of HMSO Guidance
Note 8.

Contents

Contents

Introduction

This book is designed to help you inspire children to improve their basic writing skills to the highest level of their ability. Any writing that is required of us throughout our lives needs to serve its purpose effectively, whether it be a shopping list or a job application. This book aims to offer tips and activity suggestions to help children achieve success through increasing their confidence as they develop their skill. It also seeks to increase children's personal satisfaction in their creative writing, a process which can often have cathartic value at times of emotional turmoil, such as life-changing family events.

Preparing to write

Are the pencils sharpened? Is scrap paper handy for draft work? Are the children able to help themselves to paper as they need it without disruption to others' writing and without damaging paper stocks? A practical, writer-friendly environment will influence children's attitude to writing. It is important that children know where they can gain help with spellings, punctuation and other such basics. Lists of common words – question words; time phrases and so on, are a help. An alphabet on display is a handy reminder for when children need to use dictionaries, thesauri or an index.

Celebrating the written word

A classroom that celebrates children's writing encourages the children to take pride in their own and their friends' efforts. It is good to display examples of the children's writing at their eye-level for them to read and re-read their stories, poems and reports. When their work is mounted and labelled neatly, they learn that their writing is valued. If wall-space is limited enable their words to be read through class anthologies, concertina books in the library corner, and in corridor spaces. Their 'by-line' given due prominence is important validation, to remind children that they are authors just as much as the writers of published books.

Allowing the wood to show through the trees

The National Literacy Strategy and the Literacy Hour, has provided a wonderful basis for systematic teaching of word, sentence and text level skills; the writer's tools of trade. It is easy, however, to lose sight of the purpose of gaining these skills. So now your children can write; why would anyone want to? The intention of this book is to act in advocacy for the whole rationale of the writing experience. It explores and encourages outlets for children to discover the joys of writing: conveying information, demonstrating knowledge and discoveries, putting feelings and opinions into words and indulging in flights of creative fantasy, akin to music, art and dance, through storytelling and poetry writing.

You Can... Establish a comfortable writing environment

'A poor workman blames his tools' is an old saying, but there's nothing like poor tools to act as a disincentive to producing top-quality work. A sharp pencil of adequate length and a fresh page together with enough light and elbow room invite a child to work and encourage the child to create neat and careful writing, promoting a sense of pride in the work produced.

Thinking points

● Make sure every day starts with sharp pencils, or pens that are in good repair, with one for everybody and a few spares. You could appoint a monitor to help you.

● Store paper in ways that it can be accessed easily without causing landslides or creasing to other sheets.

● Demonstrate that you value the children's work by keeping it as pristine as possible when handling it. Display examples of the children's efforts with pride. This will encourage the children to take equal pleasure in their work.

● Changes in the weather in our inimitable climate mean that cloud cover can render a classroom very dark before we have realised it. Keep an eye on the weather or appoint a lights monitor to switch lights on and off as required. Enthusiasm and effort dwindle in the gloom.

Tips, ideas and activities

● Seat children so that all have enough personal space. This will mean putting left-handed children to the left of their partner – or at the left-hand end if seated in rows.

● If the children are working on loose sheets of paper, make sure that they have something firm, but giving, to rest on. A hard table is not conducive to comfortable handwriting.

● If possible, have some clipboards to hand, so that the children may choose a quiet spot to go and do their writing in. This is particularly useful for creative writing – where children need quiet 'thinking space'. Some may find they are more creative when sitting on the carpet and resting on a cushion than in the arrangement used for more formal writing. You might even assign a Comfort Zone especially for such purposes. Clipboards are also useful for field trips or simply for use when writing outdoors around the school grounds.

● For children who are intimidated by a blank sheet of paper, make use of individual whiteboards – where changes in drafts or mistakes can be fixed easily, before being committed to paper.

● Keep scrap paper available for children to test out spellings, make notes, and so on.

● Sometimes you will want children to illustrate their writing and use plain paper. Keep a plentiful supply of lined paper, in heavy print, so that it will show through the plain paper as a guide. Paper clips, one in each corner, will help keep the guidelines in place.

● Keep your own desk tidy for your own benefit as well as for setting an example. Simple plastic trays to hold finished work awaiting marking avoid landslides of paper. You could colour-code these according to subject matter or group.

You Can... **Reduce fear of the blank page**

Even adults can feel intimidated when faced with a blank sheet of paper. Committing pen to paper can seem daunting for two reasons: one, fear of mark-making on a spotless surface, especially fear of making mistakes; two, an onset of 'writer's block' brought on by the enormity of 'damaging' a seemingly expectant surface.

Thinking points

- Demonstrate writing on a piece of blank paper for the children to observe. Often, simply writing a name and date at the top of the page is sufficient to 'break the ice'.

- Drawing a left-hand margin on a sheet of plain paper, again, acts as mark-making before 'writing proper' begins.

- The use of spider-graphs breaks up the area of paper into smaller, attainable sections. When writing non-fiction texts, use shape templates such as squares, circles and triangles to create a decent-sized space for writing.

- Folding the paper horizontally in half, and half again (and opening it out again before writing) is another way of reducing the blankness of the page. It can also help the children to divide their writing into paragraphs.

Tips, ideas and activities

- Hold up a sheet of blank paper and ask the children to picture it as the playground, covered in snow that has fallen quickly and thickly. Ask: *Who would rush to plant their footsteps? Who would hesitate to destroy the pristine surface?* Remind the children that it will snow again (this is not a once-in-a-lifetime experience). Their footprints are not only a valid addition to the snow, creating patterns and decoration, but they are their own, unique, personal signatures in the snow. Explain that, in the same way, it is 'safe' for them to begin writing.

- Create opportunities for the children to express their own thoughts and feelings in writing – with no rights or wrongs, where they need not worry about misspellings or corrections. This could be an occasional activity or a regular journal. Allocate an area of wall-space to act similarly to a blog (a 'Weblog' or online journal) – you could call it the Clog (Classroom Log) where children can pin up their comments and feelings on school and life in general. Make one side a huge sunshine and the other a big black cloud, with a neutral overlap; the children can allocate their written feelings to the appropriate mood area.

- Invite children to attempt 'automatic writing'. Give them a topic – this can be just one word (such as *sleep*; *walls*; *water*) – and ask them to begin writing immediately, the word itself and anything that it suggests to them (single words, phrases or sentences). Tell them that spelling does not matter; their aim is to allow words to flow from their pen. It may or may not lead to rewrites, developing into poems, stories or articles. Perform the same activity yourself at the same time, for the children to see. Scribe for those children that need help to get started.

You Can... Strengthen children's writing

There is a wealth of dictionaries, encyclopaedias and thesauri available for classroom use. There are also many specialist dictionaries of, for example, rhyme, etymology, phrase and fable (in traditional book format as well as online). Teaching children how to use these effectively is a gift for a lifetime's writing.

Thinking points

● The greatest means of strengthening children's writing is through exposure to exemplary writing by effective and experienced authors. Make sure that the class library is filled with well-written books, that fulfil their purpose and stretch the children's vocabulary. The books will inspire and influence the children's own efforts.

● Reference books, such as dictionaries and thesauri, are only as useful as a child's willingness and ability to use them. This involves recognition of their value to encourage them to open the cover. It also requires familiarity with alphabetical indexing, so exercises to practise arranging words alphabetically, and use of an index, are imperative.

● The word thesaurus is derived from the Greek word for treasure. Treasure is valuable. It is worth encouraging children to think of extra-special words as valuable – worth digging out in order to enrich their writing.

Tips, ideas and activities

● Encourage children to keep a personal word-log of new, valuable words as they come across them in their reading and their 'digging' in dictionaries and thesauri.

● Place an alphabet up on the wall near the reference books, for reassurance. Invite slower learners to write their own individual alphabet and stick it to their desktop for easy reference.

● Display the alphabet as a semicircle. Position each separate letter using Blu-Tack. Highlight the positions of A, M–N, and Z to show the beginning, middle and end of the alphabet. Also highlight G and T, to encourage the children to look at the separate quarters of the alphabet.

● Play observation games where letters are swapped or missing, and speed-games where all or selected letters must be positioned against the clock, until the whole class knows the alphabet backwards – and can recite it in both directions.

● Reinforce the alphabet (and enhance children's playground adventure games!) by teaching the phonetic alphabet, used internationally in the English-speaking world to avoid mistakes through mishearing: Alpha, Bravo, Charlie, Delta, Echo, Foxtrot, Golf, Hotel, India, Juliet, Kilo, Lima, Mike, November, Oscar, Papa, Quebec, Romeo, Sierra, Tango, Unicorn, Victor, Whisky, X-ray, Yankee, Zulu.

● Challenge the children to a treasure hunt. Arrange the class into pairs, providing a thesaurus between two. Give out the following words (or similar everyday verbs or adjectives) and ask them to look them up and collect a list of exciting, interesting alternatives. As verbs and adjectives add the most strength to description, begin with these. Verbs: *walk, see, say, throw, ride, hurry, jump, lift*; Adjectives: *slow, funny, sad, bright, loud, lovely, big, small.*

You Can... Promote a sense of achievement

We all enjoy doing what we're good at, so the better we can do something the more we will enjoy it. If we do it well then we get that buzz of satisfaction which is a sense of achievement. Showing children that they can achieve, and showing belief in their ability, will help them to work to their full capability. Teacher expectation is essential for a child to succeed. And nothing succeeds like success!

Thinking points

● As their teacher, your expectations of the children will influence their own self-image and expectations and, ultimately, their performance. Always expect more of them than they will actually achieve; that way they will never fall short of their potential.

● Remind children that they are competing only against themselves – is their work improving against what they were producing a month ago? Make sure children keep examples of their efforts early in the school year, so that they can compare newer work and notice improvements for themselves.

● Reassure children who are disappointed with their work that we all have off days, and find a point to praise. It is always possible to find something to commend in every child's work.

● While stretching more-able children, always tailor targets to be achievable by less-able children. For example, your expectation of a page from one child may be a paragraph from another.

Tips, ideas and activities

● Giving children a purpose for their writing will encourage them to make their best effort. Announce ahead of writing what will be the destiny of their finished piece to provide an incentive. Ideas include:
  - A page in a project book
  - Part of a classroom or corridor display, such as a Poem Wall
  - A contribution to a class anthology
  - Work for their parents to see on an open evening
  - A text to be used in assembly or read out loud
  - A story to be read or a play acted out to another group
  - A competition entry
  - A legible draft for later development
  - A poem to go inside a Mother's Day card.

● Encourage the children to experiment with creative writing straight onto the computer. Alternatively, arrange for them to transfer their work to a word-processing program, choosing font, colour, size and decoration before printing. Seeing their composition appearing, like the printed word that they see in books, reinforces recognition that books don't just 'happen' – somebody has done exactly what they have done – sat down, planned, written and rewritten. If possible, allow the children to print copies of work that they are pleased with to keep and re-read.

● Demonstrate the value of cutting and pasting (physically as well as when using a word processor) as a part of the creative, drafting process. Children will then see how they can improve their writing without laborious copying or re-keying.

● In plenary sessions, provide regular opportunities for children to read their work aloud.

You Can... Encourage children to finish their writing

Like reading stamina, writing stamina is something that builds up gradually. But where reading is largely a passive activity (unless making notes, discussing or following instructions from non-fiction texts), writing is active. As the human condition tends towards laziness, this can be an uphill struggle, especially for children who are not predisposed to sitting still and thinking.

Thinking points

● Although you may be a lover of writing yourself, it is worth remembering that to many children writing is a chore akin to tidying their bedroom or drying up. Chores are more easily done if there is a reward. These come in many guises.

● Define what you consider to be completion of work at the start of an activity so that children understand each target before they start. There may be several goals within one session – just as there are plateaux before climbing to a mountain top!

● While it is important to have high expectations of your children, try not to expect everything to come right at once – decide what are the priorities of any one lesson or exercise.

Tips, ideas and activities

● There is an old engineering maxim when quoting for work: they can produce the end result better, faster or cheaper! Select any two of these three choices for the children's writing ('cheaper' can translate as 'quantity'). That is to say, do you want the children to write more and better (but take longer over it) or more and faster (at the expense of quality – of say, spelling or vocabulary) or better and faster (more accurate, but perhaps only a sentence or two)? Expecting several pages of speedy, erudite perfection (all three) is perhaps too much!

● What will be the reward for work completed on target? Consider the following:

　● Successfully completed work is often reward in itself – the look, the sound, the feel of the thing. Ask how the applauded children feel about their achievement. Let others hear and see how it feels to be pleased with one's effort. Make your classroom a gallery to their success.

　● Champion any progress among slower children by public praise.

　● Keep individual completion bar charts for children to measure their own success. On a ten-square-high chart, the child may colour the five squares you have dotted for them, when they half-complete their task. A 100% column may earn a reward.

　　● Last but not least: bribery! This can range from house points, lots of praise and a smiley sticker to an extra five minutes' play for whole class effort or a mention in assembly, highlighting the work's merit and applauding the author.

● Doing something extra with finished work adds an incentive to complete tasks. Make this a separate session to avoid children rushing to do 'the fun bit' – adding their contribution to a display; turning their long thin poem into a bookmark, and so on.

You Can... **Provoke children's pride in their writing**

Lead by example, and practise what you preach. Show that you take a pride in your own writing. This can be demonstrated on a daily basis – your handwriting on the board, annotating displayed work, writing instructions, lists, captions, even marking the register neatly. Children will notice the care you take because you are their role model.

Thinking points

● Explain clearly to the children what you expect of them in terms of presentation and content. What do you want them to do if they make a mistake? Perhaps they put brackets around the error and add a small cross; perhaps you permit the use of erasers.

● If the appearance of work is neat it encourages children to make sure that the content lives up to the presentation. Conversely, the impact of good content is impaired if presented scruffily or illegibly. Help your children to develop good habits early on.

● Warn children in advance that they will need to be able to read their work aloud. Careful writing makes reading easier. Point out that you want to display their work with pride.

● Advise children that what they create in words is a part of them. Encourage them to use by-lines to promote a sense of ownership.

Tips, ideas and activities

● Encourage the children to choose a pen that suits their handwriting for writing up neat copies of their work. Suggest that they keep a pen for best work. Remind them to use a ruler for underlining headings or drawing margins.

● Teach the children how to use omission marks so that words left out can be written elsewhere on the page rather than squashed in illegibly.

● Create a Writers' Corner in your classroom. Divide your class into groups – for example, tables of six children. At weekly intervals, allow a group at a time to display the pieces of writing, done that week, of which they are most proud – one each. Every Friday change the display to the next group's choice. You need not announce which group's turn it will be until the Friday, to encourage widespread effort. Tell the children that every week, in addition to the group's own choices, you will select another piece of writing to display from anyone in the class (ensuring that even the group whose work has just been on display can still make the effort to win a place).

● Encourage the children to mount extra-special writing on sugar paper. A carefully ruled border line on the mount, one centimetre outside the paper's perimeter, adds a further finishing touch to reinforce a sense of pride in the finished work.

● Develop a mutual arrangement with another teacher to send children to show pieces of writing that they are particularly pleased with. This works especially well if arranged between teachers of adjacent year-groups. It retains or forges rewarding links between a past/future teacher and classroom, providing helpful insight for teachers and continuity for children. Clearly, agreement of suitable times is essential but can often be arranged during breaks to achieve spontaneity.

You Can... Inspire children to want to write

At school, as in everyday life, we have to do things we don't want to do. Being in the right mood for an activity is important if we are to make the best of a task. Your own enthusiasm (even your body language) will influence the children's approach to writing. The Literacy Hour is a great means of teaching the tools of the trade, but it should not be seen as an end in itself. Motivation and facilitation for inspired writing requires stimulating springboards and a good place to start is with the children themselves.

Thinking points

● Drawing on the children's hobbies and out-of-school activities offers instant child-centred interest. 'Write about what you know' is the advice to all would-be writers, and this will bring out the best in children's writing too. You are offering them an outlet to share their knowledge and enthusiasm with others. When the content is at the front of their mind, the mechanics of writing become less of a burden.

● Read aloud to the children, choosing works by their favourite authors. Let them immerse themselves in the text without the effort of deciphering the written word. It will help the syntax and phraseology of storytelling to become ingrained and natural in their own writing.

Tips, ideas and activities

● Invite the children to interview a partner about their interests, taking notes and writing up their interview. Swap the results and allow the partners to advise each other on accuracy or how details might be expressed more excitingly.

● Encourage the children to write a pamphlet about their own hobby, pet or a favourite participatory sport. Challenge them to provide information in such a way as to enthuse others and promote their chosen subject.

● Ask the children to write a guidebook to their school, club or town, aimed at visitors or newcomers. List possible areas to include (for a town these might include public buildings and amenities; hotels and restaurants, schools and playgroups, entertainment and clubs). Point out the value of sub-titles and bullet points to help readers to find information quickly and easily.

● Suggest that children put themselves and/or friends in their stories or locate a fictional character in a known environment. This builds on existing knowledge and increases confidence.

● Towards the end of the school year, invite children to write down something memorable about the year – a time they got into trouble but now see the funny side of how they feared the teacher before they got to know him or her; the day there was a new child or an exciting excursion. Compile children's accounts into a loose-leaf book and swap with another class to read each other's real-life stories.

● Ask the children to write about someone they know personally that they admire (that is, not a pop-singer, footballer or film-actor, unless, of course, they do know them personally!) and ask them to read their accounts aloud.

You Can... **Improve the mechanics of writing**

We have all at some time heard someone, staring in bewilderment at a piece of paper, remark, 'I can't read my own writing!' And if the writer himself can't, then what chance does anyone else have? Writing needs to match its purpose – note-making does not have to look like copper-plate, but all handwriting needs to be legible.

Thinking points

● Children's levels of motor control vary enormously and mature at different ages. Close friends will often copy not only the content of each other's writing, but the style of letter-formation, adopting each other's idiosyncrasies. Regular, formal handwriting practice can help children to develop their own 'hand'.

● Bad habits and inappropriate embellishments of letters can spread like wildfire – dots that become tiny circles can quickly grow into small planets in writing space. Allow children to embellish title-covers to topic work as an acceptable creative outlet for bubble-writing and the like.

● By the time a child is seven, how they hold their pen or pencil will be pretty well established. However, it is worth persevering in demonstrating and encouraging a comfortable grip.

Tips, ideas and activities

● Explain that handwriting must suit its purpose. Brevity, casual lettering and inaccurate spelling are fine for personal notes and drafts, or for note-making while listening to speech, but all writing needs to be legible. The aesthetics of handwriting can be saved for 'fair copies' or for letters for others to read.

● Introduce the word 'jot' as a signal to indicate when casual writing is required (writing that is for their eyes only). It must be legible, but only they will need to re-read it, such as when making notes when listening to a speaker; making notes from a longer printed source as they read. Suggest a few common abbreviations for such jottings, things such as *C19* for 'nineteenth century'; @ for 'at'; & for 'and'. Point out that they can invent other shorthand symbols of their own – as long as they don't forget them!

● Demonstrate consistent letter-formation in a formal way. Poems are a perfect vehicle for handwriting practice. Their short lines accommodate differing sizes of script, so even those with large handwriting can generally fit their letters to a line. They provide practice of upper- and lower-case letters and can also grow into an enjoyable anthology.

Remember to practise your handwriting

● Use a variation of the 'Chinese whispers' game to demonstrate legibility requirements of casual writing. Read out a shopping list for the children to 'jot' down. Give the children scrap paper or whiteboards and read your prepared list fairly quickly. Afterwards, ask them to read items from their lists with a partner. How many words can their partner decipher?

● Use photocopiable page 56 for individual handwriting practice. Alternatively, make an enlarged copying of the lower half to create a full-sized A4 handwriting guide.

You Can... Develop confidence in spelling

English is renowned for the eccentricity of its spellings. Recognising its broad sources, including Latin and Greek, helps children to accept that there are explanations and that spelling is not an arbitrary annoyance. It can become a bonus, too, when learning foreign languages, as we have so many synonyms from different linguistic roots. For example, the word bottle *is like the French,* bouteille; *and we also have the word* flask, *akin to the German word for bottle,* Flasche. *That Germanic* sch- *pattern also gives rise to our spelling of the word,* school (Schule).

Thinking points

● It is a relatively recent concept that spelling be set in concrete. Many American spellings, such as *gray*, were English two hundred years ago.

● Give credit for misspellings where they are phonetically plausible – *trane* may be incorrect, but the phonetic pronunciation of the chosen letter-string makes the meaning clear and applies the vowel-lengthening rule.

● Clarify when spelling does and does not matter. Children whose creative writing is just beginning to take off should not be thwarted. Save hurdles for when you are teaching spelling; allow a free run in the early days of training sprinters!

Tips, ideas and activities

● Remind the children that the purpose of all writing is communication. Correct spelling can avoid misunderstanding. Telling someone that they need to see a *councillor* means that they need advice on civic affairs. If they need a *counsellor* it implies they need personal help. Computer spell-checkers will not pick up misspelled homophones – only we can do that. Identifying the core word helps – in this case, *council/counsel*.

● Similarly, when we have to decide whether a word ends in *-or* or *-er* it sometimes helps to try both and decide which looks right. We can then check our decision in a dictionary. Write *jeweller* and *jewellor* and *docter* and *doctor* on a board and ask the children to decide which are right.

● Ask how children feel if someone misspells their name. Encourage the class to spell their peers' names. Develop this into a game. Write one child's name on the board. S/he comes out and writes the name of a friend. If spelled correctly, they line up and it's the named child's turn. If spelled incorrectly, the named child corrects the spelling and lines up ahead of their friend.

● Make use of and display adages as reminders: 'I before E except after C' mostly works. Children soon learn exceptions.

● Create mnemonics for any word that is persistently misspelled. This may involve making connections: 'Fri(day) ends the week, so I can play with my fri-ends', or devising a personally memorable acrostic: 'Our Nan Can Eat (ONCE)'!

● A Spelling Bee can act as an incentive to learn difficult spellings – children ask sponsors to donate an amount per correctly spelled word. A ten-word test soon tops up school funds.

You Can... Eradicate common spelling mistakes

Familiarity, example and practice all contribute to the development of accurate spelling habits. Displays reminding children of frequently used and confused spellings will impinge on their visual senses. Plentiful opportunities for private reading will help children to recognise if their attempts to spell words look right. Spelling out loud will help children with stronger aural memory. A multi-sensory approach cannot but help.

Thinking points

● Help children to make connections between words with common roots. Choosing between *there* and *their* will be easier if children notice *here* within *there* (both place words). Choices can be via elimination, too – *their* contains no place word, so it must be the possessive.

● Encourage children to recognise the meaning of prefixes and suffixes. For example, children taught that *mono* means *one* can make an informed choice in spelling *monotonous* or *monocle*.

● Practice makes perfect! (Not to be confused with *practise* the verb. *Ice* is a noun; *is* is a verb. So, *practice*: noun; *practise*: verb.) Encourage children to share mnemonics with their peers.

● 'It's the exception that proves the rule' is another old adage – handy to throw back at any bright sparks too ready to point out where the rule fails!

Tips, ideas and activities

● All children should keep a spelling log of new words and the correct spellings of regular misspellings.

● Invite children to set their own learning targets, experimenting with combined methods: look-spell-cover-write-check; repeated scribing; spelling aloud for a spelling-buddy to check.

● Target particular regular spelling rules to teach and practise with whole groups, such as -y becoming -ies for (noun) plurals, and vice versa for (verb) third-person plurals – He carr*ies* the jell*y*: they carr*y* the jell*ies*.

● Encourage the children to draw on the meanings of words to determine spelling. A common misspelling is 'seperate'. Teach children that the word *pare* means to cut; as in a *paring knife*, and the middle *a* in *separate* becomes more memorable through logic. (And if the child has never heard of a paring knife, you are extending their vocabulary too!)

● Lead by example. Make a point of openly looking up spellings in a dictionary. Share your decision-making approach to dictionary searches with the group. What, for instance, if you can't spell cyclone? It doesn't appear under S; nor under C-I-... What other ways are there? Perhaps it is like the word *cycle* as in *bicycle*... and there it is!

● Some words are frequently misspelled by adults and children alike. Hold spelling contests to encourage children to sit down and learn them – perhaps competing in groups or pairs. Concentrate on words that they are likely to have to write frequently, offering help in memorising them, such as *forty* (lose the *u* from *four*); *ninety*, (9+ty); *Wednesday* (say it phonetically: Wed-nes-day); *barbecue* (three small words bar+be+cue).

You Can... Teach children how to use punctuation

It is fairly straightforward to teach children the basics of punctuation – the 'full stop, capital letter' rule of a simple sentence; the question mark in lieu of a full-stop; using commas within lists. It is moving on from these that becomes more difficult. Even adults struggle with punctuation and the adage 'If in doubt, leave it out' is probably quite sensible. If only this applied to the infamous and ubiquitous 'greengrocer's apostrophe'!

Thinking points

● Concentrate on the most important aspects of punctuation, remembering that clarifying meaning and avoiding ambiguity are the ultimate purposes.

● Stamp on the first signs of sticking apostrophes into plurals.

● If in doubt over questions of punctuation, refer the children to any well-written published text and ask them to look for an example that answers their question. For instance, where do commas appear in direct speech – inside or outside the inverted commas? ('Inside,' they should tell you!)

Tips, ideas and activities

● Invite the children to examine reliable printed texts to look for patterns in punctuation and examine how different marks are used. Challenge them to devise a rule-book, explaining how and when to use certain punctuation. Include examples with book/page references. Check that their inferences and conclusions are accurate.

● Present children with modified texts – copying a text but omitting punctuation. Invite the children to read and make sense of this to show how difficult it is. Invite them to add the punctuation as they see fit and then check with the original. Demonstrate re-reading the text aloud more easily with the punctuation visible.

● Create enlarged texts with a supply of common punctuation marks on sticky notes for children to physically position and reposition. Invite them to explain their decisions. Encourage others to challenge errors and offer explanations.

● There are plentiful examples of the misuse of punctuation on the high street and in published material such as local papers and advertising flyers that drop through the letter box. Widespread abuse of punctuation can undermine classroom teaching, but turn this into a positive. Hold a class competition to see which group of children can report the largest number of errors that have met their eye in any one week. (You might extend this to spellings too). You will soon have a class of punctuation-obsessives. It works for Lynne Truss, author of *Eats Shoots and Leaves* – an illuminating and helpful read for anyone, especially teachers who may be put on the spot!

● Try to eradicate the incorrect apostrophe that often creeps into the possessive *its*. *It's* can *ONLY* mean 'it is' or 'it has'. Guide the children to note the possessive *his* – no apostrophe! – the same goes for its.

You Can... Offer strategies to create reader-friendly text

Children who understand their audience will more easily adapt their writing to suit the reader. Experience of reading different genres is an essential experience prior to asking children to write in different genres. Using long words per se (while to be encouraged in terms of vocabulary extension and potentially enriching description) is not always the most effective means of communication.

Thinking points

● Help children to match their style to the requirements – a sign saying *WET PAINT* may not be poetic but it works!

● Establish who the children are writing for before they begin. Explain how long their piece should be.

● Giving children a structure and target word-count will help them to pace and order the content of their writing.

● Ensure that children understand how they need to adapt their personal style of writing to meet the requirements. For example, the layout of a letter is distinctive and follows set conventions with little leeway for improvisation; the style of a story, on the other hand, is much more open.

Tips, ideas and activities

● Hold a genre comparison session within a common theme. Ideas include: road, home safety, accidents, natural history, disasters, phenomena. Give each group of six children sample texts from one of the following genres: letters; newspaper reports; fiction; instructional texts; diary or journal. Ask the children to jot down notes on style and layout, also noting any special vocabulary, or even distinctive clichés, such as 'It was alleged', 'He confessed' (newspapers). Notes might include: numbering and use of imperative verbs (instructional texts); third-person narrative and direct speech (fiction); informal abridged sentences – often omitting the first-person pronoun, 'Went to cinema' (diary/journal); formal/informal language, layout of address, date, openings/endings (letters).

● Together brainstorm an idea of a fictional event or take a real local issue relating to the chosen theme, such as fundraising and safety issues for a children's play area and its equipment. Briefly list the issues, for example: *Need to repair fence by busy road; Mend or remove dangerous equipment; Deny access to dogs; Raise money to paint seats*, and so on. Challenge each group to write reports in their designated genre and compare the results, noting how the writing style varies for the different audiences.

● Invite the children to present their writing in an appropriate layout, such as word-processing a news report in columns.

● Offer children check-points for self-assessment: Is their writing simple, direct and economical? Can they remove unnecessary words? Are their sentences short and unambiguous? Is their writing ordered and structured logically? As a rule of thumb, 15 to 20 words is as long as any sentence should be. Basically, when read aloud, that's a lungful!

You Can... Enable children to paraphrase without plagiarism

From an early age, children are required to research a wide range of subjects. Books, magazines, TV and radio broadcasts, films and internet sites all offer a wealth of information. Firstly, children must sort through and assess the credibility and reliability of information. This is a difficult enough task even before they begin to select from, and rephrase, the content. Above all, it is essential to avoid simply copying out someone else's words. Children don't like others copying their work; the same applies to grown-up professionals!

Thinking points

● No one is going to sue a schoolchild for copyright, but it is worthwhile explaining the basic concept of 'ownership of words' and plagiarism, especially as we encourage children to feel a sense of ownership.

● Developing the art of précis and note-taking will help force children to rephrase sentences.

● Use of a thesaurus to provide synonyms is helpful where the essence of a sentence needs retaining but there is little scope for paraphrasing.

● Model how direct quotations may be used and acknowledged – either within text, or as a footnote. This choice will depend on the purpose and length of the piece and the quantity and frequency of quotation-use.

Tips, ideas and activities

● Find examples of texts on a chosen subject including, if possible, internet texts, using an interactive whiteboard. Demonstrate ways of note-making, for example:
  ● Using a highlighter (or text selection tool) to pick out key information. In the case of text on a computer, you may also demonstrate use of the word-search tool within text.
  ● Modelling bullet-point note-making from lengthy sentences or paragraphs, noting only the essential words and concepts, names and dates, as appropriate.
  ● Finding simple sentences in clauses and parentheses.

● Show how subtitles can organise notes into a logical order that may be translated into paragraphs. For example, when researching Wolves, headings might be: habitat; social structure; food and hunting; breeding; lifespan; conservation.

● Use the sample text on photocopiable page 57 to show how notes may be taken and texts rewritten, combined and/or embellished without straight copying.

● Choose a text to read twice to the children, asking them to listen the first time and take notes the second. Ask questions about the text and invite the children to use their notes to supply answers, encouraging full sentences. Compare these with the original text. Have they successfully reworded the text while retaining the gist of the meaning?

● Challenge children to write their own non-chronological information text on, for example, Wolves. Encourage them to conduct further research to add to an original draft.

● As the children's accounts will certainly overlap and contain duplicate information, compare how different children have worded similar information. Write anonymous examples on the board to read side by side. Are some better than others and, if so, why? Are they all good but different in style?

You Can... Monitor children's self-assessment

For children to progress they need to know what they are doing right as well as what they are doing wrong. We may assume that we have made our requirements clear, but children can misunderstand or misinterpret what we say. Clarification of aims, and assessment and agreement of how far those aims have been met, helps both child and teacher to achieve.

Thinking points

● Children will write better if they know precisely what is expected from them. Always explain the target clearly and how they must set about achieving it. Asking a child to repeat your requirements in their own words will help to ensure that you have a mutual understanding of targets.

● While always checking that their writing matches its purpose, try not to assess too many specifics at the same time; choose one focus.

● Devise a marking system that shows children their mistakes as well as their successes, while avoiding the humiliating and soul-destroying scored red lines. Try using an alerting red-pen asterisk to identify an area for comment, reserving black, blue or green ink for the comment itself – positive or negative.

● In plenary sessions, encourage the children to make affirmative self-assessment statements, such as, 'I can find and use interesting adjectives.'

Tips, ideas and activities

● Use copies or adaptations of photocopiable page 58 to suit your needs. Encourage the children to make self-assessments of their work. Follow this up with your own assessment when marking their writing. Attach these forms to examples of work, providing evidence of learning and performance, and contributing to record-keeping and continuing evaluation. This information will make it easier to identify which problems need addressing on a whole class, small group or individual level, and which areas of writing are secure.

● Ask the children to underline examples of where they think they have succeeded in their writing task. For example, they may underline each strong verb used to create a more vivid description. You may then add a tick of agreement or, say, a question mark over banal verbs that could have been stronger, providing instant feedback. Used in conjunction with all writing activities on a regular basis this reminds the children to check their writing for sense, punctuation, spelling and so forth – a good habit for life.

● Mutual understanding of targets will be revealed and reinforced during plenary sessions when the children can assess themselves and each other in a positive, supportive way. A child who has been able to underline lots of effectively used vivid verbs will share them with increasing pride and confidence. Less-able children will also learn from their mistakes and from others' achievements.

● When assessing it is worth taking notes of children's spoken comments about their own and others' work. Their observations often reveal their level of understanding and whether their learning is secure. Inviting children to explain why they wrote something in a certain way, or chose a particular word, also goes a long way to divulging their degree of comprehension.

You Can... Introduce the cathartic value of writing

Whether it's walking the dog or playing loud music, we all need an outlet for our frustrations. Writing can be therapeutic and children may find that penning their feelings helps them to deal with problems, release tensions and possibly even reach conclusions. Writing can also be used to communicate feelings to others which are hard to put into spoken words, or writing can simply help people to understand their own feelings.

Thinking points

● Encouraging children to recognise and deal with their feelings will help them to cope with difficulties and channel their emotions. Once, I noticed a ten-year-old, self-controlled boy write something rapidly on a piece of scrap paper, immediately screw it up, slam it into the waste-paper bin and return to his seat. He then carried on seamlessly with his work. After the children had gone home, I retrieved the paper. 'I hate Lisa,' was all it said – but it had served its purpose and no one, not even the offending girl, was hurt.

● When a child is clearly upset but won't say why, suggest that they write down how they feel. Allow them to keep this private unless they invite you to read it.

Tips, ideas and activities

● A release of feelings may be encouraged during free-writing sessions. Ask the children to write about a time when they were aware of a strong emotion – anger, fear, a surge of love or hate, elation, sadness. Results may range from being unfairly grounded, to more life-challenging moments such as the death of a family member.

● When a child does write something that moves them, help them to decide what they would like to do with the written piece. They may simply want to keep it. Sometimes they may want to rework their initial outpouring of words as a prose-poem and add a dedication, or type it up on the computer, printing it in a fitting border. They might want to take it home. Encourage the children to decide what would be appropriate.

● If the whole class is upset about something – a council threat to close the local park, for example, help them to channel their feelings into a formal protest, such as a well-constructed letter presenting their argument. (Check with the headteacher before sending their protest to the relevant bodies.)

● Frustration can build up in children if people who control aspects of their life will not listen to them. Children can feel exasperated and helpless in the lack of control they have over their own lives. One eight-year-old girl desperately wanted a pet. Her parents were not keen on the idea of caged animals and felt the responsibility too much for her. Determined to achieve her ambition, the child expressed her rationale in writing; anticipating potential pitfalls and demonstrating her knowledge of hamster care! The result – her parents allowed her to have a pet hamster and never regretted it. The power of the written word cannot be underestimated, even when the writer is under 11.

You Can... **Build confidence in creative writing**

Writing creatively can be a liberating experience, once the writer learns to 'let go'. Children are less inhibited than adults at giving their imagination free rein. Sometimes, however, stories can stray too far from reality. Invention is great, fantasy is fun, but it is important that fiction remains plausible.

Thinking points

● Point out the power children possess as creative writers: they can invent characters, situations, places that don't exist. They can make people – including themselves – do and say things that they never could in real life.

● Unlike in maths, for example, there are no right or wrong answers. Creative writers are in control; they decide what happens. They can use creative writing as escapism, entertainment, revenge to redress the unfairness of real life or even as a soap-box to project a point of view.

● Remind the children that however implausible a world the writer creates, characters and events need to be plausible within that world.

Tips, ideas and activities

● The old maxim 'Write about what you know' pertains for children, too. Putting themselves and their friends in a story instantly provides characters with genuine hopes, fears, problems and ambitions. They may change the names, the genders and write in the third person, but real life easily provides characters, settings and situations.

● Creativity is the process of manipulating what you know. One children's writer defined this as 'I remember... plus Let's pretend...'. I call it the 'What if...?' factor. It leads from the known to the unknown via the imagination. Any everyday situation can begin a story. 'What if... when I rounded the corner home from school my house wasn't there?'; or 'What if... I looked in the mirror and saw ... a spotty rash; a different face; my own face glowing green...?'

● Even if character and setting are familiar, the plot will be invented or, at the very least, embellished. List question words, reminding the children to continue asking themselves throughout their planning: Why? What? Where? Who? When? How?

● Through detail, stories become realistic and convincing. Remind the children to describe their characters' appearances. This is best presented gradually, rather than forcing a straight description into one dedicated paragraph. For example, the writer might say, 'She flicked her purple hair out of her eyes' during a paragraph focusing on an action or event.

● Explain the need for plausibility within a fantasy setting. For example, in a story about some talking fish and their struggles within an ocean world, it will not do to have the main fishy character suddenly able to grow legs and walk away from a problem. It's a cop-out! If the young writers would be disillusioned reading such plots, then they should not get away with writing them!

You Can... Show the benefit of sharing ideas

Whole class brainstorming and writing is a great way of building confidence and generating ideas. Many successful TV programmes are written by teams of writers or writing partners. Writers can spin ideas off each other and develop clearer ideas. The same happens in writers' circles – when writers discuss their difficulties and resolve plot hurdles. Even JK Rowling admits to having come up against a plotting anomaly which she discussed and resolved with her editor. Sometimes 'two heads are better than one'!

Thinking points

● Any group of people working together closely on a daily basis will inevitably influence each other. This is how movements develop in the arts generally – the Impressionists of the art world and the Bloomsbury Set among writers, for example. Encourage children to think in a similar vein when it comes to sharing creative ideas.

● Brainstorming techniques and word-association activities will have benefits in other areas of the curriculum – encouraging lively open-mindedness and lateral thinking.

● Have the courage to experiment with ideas. Remind the children that draft work is essential to the creative process: changes can be made; what you write together – or individually – is not carved in stone!

Tips, ideas and activities

● Present the children with a simple character and then follow these steps:
  ● Invite suggestions as to the character's main ambition. For example: John who wants to fly. Decide on genre: Real life? Fantasy? Historical? Anthropomorphic? Fairy tale?
  ● Invite suggestions of an obstacle that John must overcome that prevents him achieving his ambition. Too young? His wings haven't grown or are broken (John doesn't have to be human!)? Father forbids him?
  ● Brainstorm ways around the problem. Through the help of another character? Through personal determination? By inventing a flying machine? Or does he fail in his quest *but* gain something else? (A different but fulfilling talent? An encounter opening new avenues in his life?)

● Through sharing ideas, the children will quickly realise that their scope is only as limited as their imaginations. They will think more widely and realise that making choices is the next stage of a storytelling process. Stress that no choice is right or wrong – all are valid.

● Either model the drafting process to make specific teaching points or ask the children, having shared ideas, to write individually, choosing to select or reject ideas discussed, and adding more ideas and new directions of their own.

● In a separate session, invite the children to read out their stories so far, and explain how the story will continue and conclude. Invite suggestions and comments from other children. Advise children who are not sure how to end their story to listen to others' suggestions. This happens in adult writers' circles all over the world. As long as children can build up mutual trust within their group, it can work for them too.

You Can... Enhance the links between reading and writing

While being taught so many aspects of the mechanics of writing – spelling, punctuation, layout, and so on – children could be tempted into believing that style itself can be learned. Their own reading habits will certainly contribute to their narrative technique, at the very least subliminally. As with pupils of the great masters of art, ultimately, their own unique voice will emerge.

Thinking points

● The wider the children's reading experience, the broader their own writing will develop and grow.

● Keeping a log of favourite and new words met in personal reading will reinforce children's active vocabulary.

● Writing book reviews encourages and helps children to analyse what it is they do or don't like about an author's style. Encourage the children to seek out more books by favourite authors.

● Close reading forces children to observe how authors achieve effects – filling out characters, creating realistic and idiosyncratic speech, achieving atmospheric description.

Tips, ideas and activities

● Explain to the children that when writing stories they must aim to set the tone in their opening sentence. For a fairy tale, it is fine to begin, *Once upon a time...* but invite children to investigate and jot down openings to stories in other genres. Together, list various types of opening, including: 1. Direct speech, often 'eavesdropping' on a conversation, 2. Description of a location, 3. Description of character(s), 4. A thematic statement.

● Read out the following examples of story openings and discuss what information is told and what is shown:

  ● *'It's no good telling me to stay off school,' said Sam, 'I'm not letting a stupid cold stop me winning the cup.'*
  Told: nothing. Shown: Sam is of school age; has a cold; is competitive.

  ● *Just past the old school, hidden behind a copse overgrown with brambles, is a huge empty house which most people in Wraithton have forgotten exists.*
  Told: Where there is a house; that it is empty. Shown: The house is in a place called Wraithton; it has been empty for some time (brambles; people have forgotten it).

  ● *There were five members of Snicker's gang and only four cans of cola between them. It was oppressively hot in the air-raid shelter and none of them felt like sharing.*
  Told: How many gang members. where they were; temperature; Shown: Snicker is the leader (use of possessive); tension between characters (none felt like sharing).

  ● *Loyalty to a friend should be the easiest thing in the world. Yet, sometimes, it is far from easy.*
  Told: an opinion. Shown: nothing.

● Challenge the children either to choose one of these beginnings and continue the story or adopt one style of opening and substitute their own ideas.

You Can... Offer children a new identity through writing

Seeing things from a different point of view is not always easy. Trying to write the thoughts and feelings in the persona of somebody other than ourselves forces us to examine their situation more closely. Whether it's a famous historical figure, an anonymous scarecrow, an alien from another planet or the man next door, we have to get inside that character's head and look at the world through a different pair of eyes.

Thinking points

● Ensure that there are biographical and autobiographical texts available in your class library for children to compare 'what makes people tick'.

● A class debate where children must argue the opposite to what they think or believe themselves obliges them to contemplate a different mindset.

● Roleplay between a variety of characters helps children's awareness of diversity. It can reveal how even unpleasant characters have some redeeming features.

● Fictional characters, once established, can be used and reused in story-writing. Famous authors do it all the time. Even apparently new characters have often simply changed names and location – the plot may only differ superficially. Challenge children to 'spot the character-types' (often stereotypes) in books by the same author. Compare Roald Dahl's Charlie and Fantastic Mr Fox; both rise above their disadvantages to conquer and outwit the cruel, egocentric or greedy opposition.

Tips, ideas and activities

● Ask the children to imagine, interview or research a character, depending on whether the character is real or imaginary. Suggest that they compile a short 'factfile' for that character: likes and dislikes; basic statistics such as age, looks, temperament; what makes them happy/annoyed, and so on.

● A fun way to approach writing in the persona of the chosen character is to use the hot-seat technique. Both the child in the hot-seat and the interviewers will gain an insight into the character. Model how to ask open questions of the child in the hot-seat. For example, 'What sort of things make you laugh?' (Rather than, 'Do you have a sense of humour?'– a closed yes/no question.)

● As children 'get to know' their character, they may experiment with writing in a range of genres, all within that persona: a page from their diary (maybe an alien's diary, while visiting Earth); a letter home (perhaps from a wartime evacuee); a newspaper interview with the character (such as a famous footballer, a TV celebrity or an unknown figure who makes the news). Such writing exercises help to establish the character in the child's mind. The letter, diary or interview may simply be 'a way in' to a character, who is now ready to walk into a fresh setting or plot another day. Alternatively, it can itself form the opening of a story.

● The advantage of thoroughly researching and planning a character is that children become more confident at writing in the first person. They can make that character do whatever they, as author, choose it to do, effectively wearing a new skin themselves. This can be liberating and fun.

You Can... **Encourage extended writing**

Writing stamina, like reading stamina, comes with practice. The hardest thing about extended writing in the classroom seems to be fitting it in among so many other things. An after-school writing club can help, as can encouraging children to continue their story-writing as homework.

Thinking points

● Writing stories in short chapters breaks extended writing into achievable chunks.

● A number of children's books are episodic in nature, effectively short stories revolving around the same characters, such as Paddington Bear, or the Sniff stories by Ian Whybrow. Adopting such an approach can help children with shorter writing stamina.

● With desktop publishing – even simply using a spiral-binder and printing on both sides of A4 paper, children can design a cover and see a finished book, adding blurb to the back cover. This 'finished product' is a great incentive to children to persevere. Add copies to the class library!

Tips, ideas and activities

● When wanting children to write a longer story, in chapters, give them a chapter word-count challenge. This will help them to pace their story across several chapters. It will also act as an incentive to break down the whole into smaller segments.

● Try getting groups of six children to plan a story between them. Each chapter's content must be planned, including how it will begin and end. Each group member, in parallel, then drafts one chapter. In a subsequent session, group members read their chapters in sequence to the rest of the group. An appointed scribe notes any continuity glitches while individual writers annotate their draft with any adjustments prior to rewrites. Planning opening lines of each chapter before they begin writing helps the flow.

● Allow individual children to emulate episodic-style story authors, writing short stories and then joining them together. Encourage the children to create an additional storyline to link the episodes. For example, consider the same central character who, in the first story, misses a bus with awkward consequences; in the second, bakes a cake which goes wrong, and in the third, learns to ride a unicycle with hilarious results. Discuss with the child, what are the underlying circumstances, hopes and fears of this character. Has he, say, fallen out with his best friend and wants to make up? Does he need to raise money for something and succeeds in the end? Show children how this extra thread can link the stories together with a little massaging of text, to create a short novel from a few short stories.

● Bringing these elements together into an extra, culminating chapter, further extends the children's writing while demonstrating how to tie in loose ends to provide a satisfying ending for the reader.

You Can... **Overcome fears of failure**

When we are born we can do nothing except by instinct. As we grow we learn. Some learning becomes instinctive so that we can act without thinking. Once we can control what we do, we are on the road to success. No one succeeds without endeavour. No one tries without motivation. It is our job to motivate children and sustain that motivation even when a child feels overwhelmed.

Thinking points

● Children should never be made to feel failures, but, as they are naturally competitive, it will happen by default. Encourage children to compare their work against their own achievements last week, not against those of their peers today.

● The worst feeling of failure for a child is when they know they have made the effort, but still feel dissatisfied. Remind children that 'tomorrow is another day'. Remind them of what they have done well. Ask them to tell you something they are pleased with, however small.

● If children are not succeeding as you think they ought, check for physical reasons: Can they hear all right? Can they see clearly? Sometimes disorders can be overlooked as children are past-masters at disguising and compensating for such problems.

● Fear of failure breeds failure. By showing confident expectation in their ability, children will feel more confident themselves and achieve more.

Tips, ideas and activities

● When you give children instructions for an activity, ask individuals prone to failure to repeat to you what they think is required of them. This removes the risk of misunderstanding or ambiguity.

● Differentiate for different ages and ability levels so that expectations, although always higher than the child will actually achieve (in order that they don't under achieve) are realistic and attainable. Break more complicated activities into smaller chunks – for example, in story-writing, a paragraph at a time.

● Ensure that children who are struggling with reading and writing have props and aids close up. For example, if they are to copy from the board, an individual version on the table in front of them encourages them to locate their place and keep up. Once children get left behind, they grow too despondent to bother.

● Allow less-confident children to work with a partner. As previously mentioned, bouncing ideas off each other oils the creative cogs.

● Teach children storyboarding techniques, providing structures for story development. Plot is often the biggest stumbling block to children. Use copies of photocopiable page 59 to help children to organise their writing plan.

● Regularly model how to set about creative writing. For children who are natural writers and enjoy and succeed at the activity, whole class shared writing may become tedious. Try using a flipchart or portable whiteboard to model writing, or act as scribe with small groups of struggling writers. Meanwhile, more-able class members can enjoy an opportunity to develop their talent without interruption.

You Can... Facilitate clear self-expression

The term 'self-expression' as used here covers everything from 'finding one's own voice' to avoiding typos. Ultimately it means clarity of writing in order to achieve clarity of understanding and conveyance of thoughts as intended. Unless a writer can transfer what is in their head to the head of the reader, they fall short of clear self-expression.

Thinking points

● Re-reading what we have written reveals errors and clumsy syntax that blurs meaning.

● Reading aloud to another person reveals if what we have written is clear. Does the reader's understanding of what we have written match what we intended to say? If not, why not? How can it be improved?

● Asking the writer, *When you wrote x, did you mean y?* is the simplest way of assessing intent and measuring success.

● Clear self-expression does not necessarily mean picking the best words or even spelling them correctly. It is a measure of whether the intended meaning comes across.

Tips, ideas and activities

● Arrange the children into small groups. Ask them to take it in turns to tell each other a story. This can be original or previously heard or read. It can be true or invented – a recent event or a distant happening; involving themselves or others. A tale can hang on something as trivial and everyday as 'My journey to school'. It could even be a fairy tale.

● At the close of the story, another member of the group must retell the same story. If there are any differences, the other children can point these out and ask for clarification from the original storyteller.

● Use these oral sessions as a forerunner to planning and writing a story. After writing, encourage the children, not only to re-read and check their work, but to read it aloud for signs of clunky phrasing. Reading aloud is particularly effective in showing up: poor punctuation, sentences that are too long or lose direction, close repetition or overuse of the same word, inadvertent change of tense or person, misapplication of pronouns.

● Ask children to mark errors and changes in different-coloured ink or pencil on their original draft. Advise them to type the finished story, incorporating any amendments, into a word-processing program where they can cut and paste, spell-check, indent paragraphs and so on.

● Remind children of the limitations of spell-checkers. These will most likely not notice the use of a wrong word if the error is itself a real word. For example, if the child has typed *The went* the program may well not alert them to the missing *y*. If they have written *Their is no mistake*, however, many programs will automatically correct the misuse of *their* to *there*. The bottom line is: checking yourself, with your own eyes and brain, is the most failsafe method.

You Can... Increase children's sense of ownership

Some years after visiting their school, I was approached in a book shop by two girls. I professed to remembering them as well as they remembered me. 'And do you remember any of the poems from that day?' I asked, thinking to contribute to a personal survey of which of my poems were most popular. 'Oh, yes!' they said. 'That jungle poem. It was brilliant!' It was the poem that we had written together during my workshop – when we put the children in the poem!

Thinking points

● Poems are about people. Even poems apparently about nature or buildings or events – all reflect people and people's viewpoints; the poets' viewpoints, as they attempt to show the world from a new angle.

● Serious poems are often about feelings. Getting across to someone how you feel is even more difficult than showing someone what you see or hear. Developing an understanding of and familiarity with poetic devices builds up a box of tools for lifelong use.

● Young children like rhyme. It is an essential element of our culture and our literary heritage. Don't be afraid to allow children to enjoy rhyme – they have the whole of their lives to explore the nuances and subtleties of less overt poetic patterning.

Tips, ideas and activities

● A Jungle Jumble or Zany Zoo is a fun way of acquainting children with alliteration, rhythm and rhyme. It is a memorable way, too, if you put the children in the poem. Possession is nine-tenths of the poem!

● At first it seems easy: children note the first *sound* of their name. They must then think, firstly, of a wild animal whose name begins with the same sound; secondly, of a verb that begins with the same sound. So, for example, Charlotte could choose *shark* and *shimmying* but not *chimpanzee* or *chortling*. Note, also, the use of present participle. This *-ing* ending prolongs the action, making it more immediate. Explain that this is going to be a light, humorous poem, so the pictures that we aim to create should be visually comical.

  ● Stanzas are built up across four lines, for example:
  Richard is reading to a reindeer
  Charlotte's shimmying with a shark
  Chloe is cooking for koalas
  Peter takes a penguin to the park.

  ● The above example has already involved editing – not as easy as it first appears. Children must learn to save rhymes for the ends of lines; juggle words to fit the rhythm (ending lines 2 and 4 with single syllables); sometimes omitting articles, such as *a*, by pluralising (*koalas*); using an apostrophe to save the *is* syllable.

  ● Repeatedly reading draft-work aloud helps establish and retain rhythm. (Incidentally, using a shark in a jungle poem introduces the notion of 'poetic licence'!)

  ● Write a stanza altogether and then invite individuals or groups to add more.

  ● Try dividing the stanzas with a refrain such as *Down in the jungle/Deep in the jungle/Don't go there alone!* – an essential and enjoyable part of the oral tradition.

You Can... **Use confidence-building exercises**

As poetry is essentially an oral art, speaking and listening to poetry being well read, recited or performed is the best way to train the ear to poetic cadence. Iambic pentameter, so favoured by Shakespeare in his sonnets and plays, lends itself to English speaking patterns, so comes easily to our collective linguistic ear. This is not to suggest that young children will write in this or any other specified form, rather that their ear will begin to recognise what sounds pleasing.

Thinking points

● Try to begin and close any poetry writing session with a reading of a poem or two as a warm up.

● Encourage children to learn poems by heart to recite individually or chorally. They will be a lifelong resource and, as they recite verse, they feel the rhythm for themselves and discover how such devices as rhyme make the words more memorable.

● The mutual support of reciting poems together will build confidence. Where there is strong rhyme or a chorus, the children anticipate what is coming so can all join in without hesitation.

● Modelling and writing poems as a class offers an excellent springboard for children individually, or in pairs or groups, to add further stanzas.

Tips, ideas and activities

● Put the children into an oral poem in which they all participate. Involving them keeps their interest and makes them want to join in. Try a rap, using the school or group's name (so the poem is unique to them!).

  ● To avoid children losing the rhythm, write the words on the board with marks above the words or syllables to be stressed. Demonstrate and practise how to 'swallow' the unstressed syllables.

  ● Introduce each child's name into the poem as you point to them, along these lines:
  Teacher: My name is X and I like to rap.
  All (chorus): Clap, clap, the Class 4 rap.
  First child: My name is Y and I like to rap.
  All: Chorus.
  Continue moving around the class until every child has added their line, attempting to retain the rhythm.

  ● Challenge the children to continue the rap, working in groups, first modelling how further rhyming couplets can be created, such as:
  I rap all night and I rap all day,
  I'll keep on rapping till we go and play.
  I rap at home and I rap at school –
  If I can't rap then I don't feel cool.

  ● Remember, you are not aiming here to create great poetry, simply to loosen up the children's thinking processes, develop a feel for rhythm and boost confidence, before setting pen to paper.

● Encourage children to paraphrase existing poems, beginning by simple substitution, such as:
The dove and the elephant flew away,
In a beautiful sky-blue plane.
They took some jelly as well as the telly,
But sent it ahead by train.

You Can... Engender children's belief in their own ability

We don't know what we can do till we try. Children will be more willing to have a go at writing a poem if they can see a way in to the activity. Given a structure, it is far easier to believe there's a chance of success. This is why making substitutions or writing parodies of poems is a helpful and popular way to start. It is a useful forerunner to providing an open structure.

Thinking points

● Painting by numbers will not produce a work of art but, with careful application, it will result in a pleasing picture, a sense of achievement and a grasp of some basic elements of painting. In the same way, writing to a formal structure will help children to find a 'way in' to poetry.

● Structure has always been used by professional poets. From simple rhyming couplets grow classical sonnets!

● A basic structure forces the writer to choose words carefully, for meaning, sound and syllable count: all ingredients of successful poems.

● Having a structure makes the writer feel 'safe' – like a fell-walker having a map – enabling them to meander from the path and find fascinating new viewpoints on the way, without getting lost.

Tips, ideas and activities

● A favourite and fairly free structure is the acrostic: the letters of the subject matter, such as F-I-R-E-W-O-R-K-S are written vertically, each line beginning with each respective letter (Fountains of stars/Iridescent in the night... and so on.)

● Writing haiku, seventeen-syllable poems of three lines, of 5-7-5 syllables respectively, encourages children to choose words for their rhythmic component. Writing these encourages children, having decided what they want to say, to look for synonyms to achieve the required syllabic pattern. As this Japanese form is traditionally inspired by seasonal aspects of nature, taking the current season as a springboard works well. It also gets children in touch with their senses – especially if they can be taken on a nature walk first.

● Repetition is a frequently occurring component of poetry and repeated opening phrases help steer children into writing economically rather than simply dividing prose into short lines.
　● Use personal experiences and memories where each stanza follows the variant pattern:
　Here is a place where I love to go (be/come/play/sleep)
　Where...
　Where...

● Invite the children to write a humorous 'Bad Week' poem of seven couplets:
On Monday I jumped out of bed,
Missed my slippers; bumped my head.
Demonstrate how, once the first person is established, the personal pronoun can be dropped – as in *(I) missed my slippers*.
● Experiment with question-and-answer poems, with or without rhyme. You could invite an alliterative component. For example:
Q: Where does the wind blow?
A: It tears through the trees.
Q: Where do the trees grow?
A: High on hairy hills.
Q: Who did you see there?

You Can... **Help children to write more expressively**

Many attempts have been made over the years to define 'what is a poem'. The one element that I believe all poems contain, however subtle, is rhythm. Whether rhyming or non-rhyming, in stanzas or otherwise, without rhythm I find it hard to define writing as other than prose. Meanwhile, without using artificial or elevated language, expression can be greatly enhanced by the use of imagery: similes, metaphor and personification.

Thinking points

● Everybody has felt cold some time in their lives. Not everybody has felt *as cold as a polar bear's pyjamas* – new, imaginative, unique imagery is a challenge worth attempting.

● We bring our own feelings and experience to every new thing we see or do. This makes our view of the world unique. Poetry is a splendid vehicle for telling others how we see things and how we feel.

● White as snow; warm as toast – traditional similes quickly become trite but, with practice, thinking up new ones is as easy as watching TV!

Tips, ideas and activities

● What if you could not see colours? Blind, or even colour-blind, people don't have a full understanding of colour. Yet colours affect, and may indeed reflect, our moods and our feelings. Challenge children to describe colours through imagery. Simile: *Red is like flames of fire*; Metaphor: *Blue is a still lake beneath a summer sky*; Personification: *Yellow wraps its arms around us in a warm cuddle.*

● How can we express emotions? If I say I feel sad, will others understand? The sadness of breaking a favourite pencil is very different from the sadness of a death in the family, so the words, *I am sad,* suddenly convey very little. Writing about the person who is no longer there, what they did with you when they were alive, will show the contrasting sadness of their loss. Describing the new pencil and how if felt and smelt or the first thing you drew with it, will reflect a different kind of loss and sadness.

● Help children to find a suitable style to match their subject. In the example above, making a comic poem about a broken pencil might be appropriate – perhaps a limerick. This would, of course, be a most inappropriate form for a serious, sad poem.

● Invite children to think of a time when they felt a strong emotion or extreme feeling: very cold; happy; tired; excited; humiliated; confused; angry; lonely. Ask them to think up a new metaphor or simile to emphasise their feeling. If their choices are trite (*as cold as ice; thrilled to bits*) encourage them to extend or adapt them (*as cold as a penguin's ice-cream; as thrilled as wedding confetti*).

You Can... Persuade children to write faster

Speed is not essential to everything in life, but there are occasions when time is limited. Getting children to realise that time is not a limitless resource is no bad thing. Certainly, when it comes to writing in a SAT they will need to speed up. Children full of ideas will have no difficulty cracking on with their poem, but others may need an added incentive.

Thinking points

● Motivation can come in many forms, but it needs putting in place ahead of the activity, with reminders during the activity to sustain steady progress.

● Walking around the class making audible observations of admiration at the amount written will help spur on others to impress you equally. Sitting at your desk involved in a separate activity tends to communicate less urgency.

● Daydreamers who are easily distracted from the task in hand may benefit from sitting in smaller groups or, occasionally, alone to develop concentration skills.

Tips, ideas and activities

● Poetry demands to be read aloud, and poetry writing activities should always close with readings. Announce in advance that only children who have finished their poem (or at least their first draft – giving you leeway for discretion and differentiation!) will be able to perform their poem.

● When drafting early stages of a poem or brainstorming ideas, establish tight time limits and 'pencils down' orders before listening to results. This sets the tone for speed early in the activity and promotes faster thinking processes as children aim to be ready for the next stage of working up ideas.

● Create a further stage of development, beyond the physical writing, that only those who have finished will be able to do. Some follow-ups may well involve all children, fast or slow alike, but, nevertheless, will encourage children to see their work displayed sooner rather than later. For example:

  ● Print and mount a long thin poem. Add a tassel to turn it into a bookmark.
  ● Create a 'thank you' poem to go inside a greetings card ready for an occasion when it's needed.
  ● Write a poem about a swan, a boat, or a hat – the subject matter of any simple origami design for the children to fold. They can then write a fair copy of their poem on the paper model itself. These make an attractive, tactile 3-D display which the children enjoy picking up to re-read. (Avoid aeroplanes!)
  ● Write a poem about a festival to hang on a tree. Provide appropriate shapes (eggs, stars, baubles, rockets and so on), a hole-punch and lengths of wool.
  ● Challenge the children to turn that day's school dinner menu into a poem. Allow early finishers to present their poem as a menu to stand on the dinner tables by noon the same day.

You Can... **Shape children's writing**

With the advent of computers and word processing, playing with text becomes irresistible. However, it always annoys me to see the words of a poem arbitrarily centred unless that was the poet's intention. Shape is part of a poem, its visual rather than oral impact, and should be a deliberate choice. Centring text appeals when the poem is a concrete poem, shaped to coincide with its subject matter.

Thinking points

● Centred lines of print lend themselves to shapes that can be shown to have a vertical central line of symmetry: a pine tree, a lit candle, a rocket, a house, a guitar, a vase.

● Shape poems that do not lend themselves to centring – and may be easier handwritten – are asymmetrical shapes: a worm, a crescent moon, a hand.

● A concrete poem is still first and foremost a poem and should be composed and drafted ahead of shaping, drawing on all the usual tools available to the poet for sound and meaning. Words can be modified to fit the shape at a later stage.

Tips, ideas and activities

● Hold up an open page from a poetry book in front of the class. Ask if they can tell you what genre of writing they are looking at. Most will guess poetry largely from its shape and its layout: short lines, often in little groups (stanzas), sometimes with inset verses (chorus), sometimes with the by-line at the end.

● Ask the children, whether rewriting a story or prose text in short lines in groups of four would turn it into a poem. Why not? Discuss use of language – poetic devices such as rhythm, alliteration and rhyme. Discuss the rationale of line breaks: to make the reader pause; to add emphasis and weight to certain words – especially one word with a line to itself; to emphasise rhythm and rhyme patterning.

● Show the children examples of concrete poems. Ask them to experiment with a pencil and plain scrap paper at writing a worm or snake poem, or something equally simply shaped. Explain that they must draft their words *before* writing them in a shape.

● As a whole class modelling exercise, try writing a poem about a cloud. Divide the class into groups, each with a thesaurus.

○ Collect keywords to describe the cloud: *big, grey, heavy, dark, wet, scary.* Allocate one word to each group for them to look up synonyms. Begin to create the cloud shape, simply by putting together pairs of descriptive words by poetic choice, such as *gloomy, looming* (assonance); *dark and dismal* (alliteration), *lumpy, bumpy* (rhyme), ending with the one word: *Cloud.*

○ When you have built up your cloud shape, emonstrate how you can develop this beyond simple description: Add the words *From a* above the cloud and make a strip of writing to hang vertically from beneath the cloud, saying *one raindrop.* And there you have it: one creative concrete cloud! (See diagram left.)

From a

o
n
e

r
a
i
n
d
r
o
p

You Can... **Have fun with words**

Playing with words is not only fun but it provides spelling practice and increases phonic awareness. It often appeals to less-able children just as much as more-able, as they begin to realise its possibilities. There may be ways of improving the spelling of a nonsense word to encourage the reader to pronounce it as intended by the writer, but no one can say a made-up word is wrong. What a liberating exercise for the reluctant writer!

Thinking points

● Shakespeare loved puns and invented words. Lewis Carroll, Edward Lear and Spike Milligan delighted in nonsense. There is plenty of precedence for wordplay in our literary heritage.

● Find and share some examples of jokes that rely on wordplay, puns and nonsense talk. Encourage the children to add their own favourites to a class collection.

● Find examples of different kinds of nonsense poem and wordplay before asking the children to determine how the nonsense is achieved and how it is used to create humour.

Tips, ideas and activities

● There are two kinds of nonsense poem:
  ● Those created through illogical use of language and impossible concepts such as:
  One fine day in the middle of the night,
  Two dead men got up to fight.
  and nonsensical syntax – such as 'verbing a noun'!
  For example:
  I scissor my nails with cutters,
  I comb my hair with a brush,
  I stair down leaps,
  And horn my beeps,
  For now I town to rush.
  (Note how one of the lines above makes sense, where *comb* and *brush* are interchangeable because they can both be a verb or a noun.)
  ● Those created through playing with words within logical syntax, such as: entirely invented words (*splog, plinkendrop*) and portmanteau words, created by splicing two halves of real words to create one new word that, in meaning, combines elements of the original words (*funnelicious = funny + delicious*); puns, often using homophones (*Good Knight, Sleep tight!*); spoonerisms – where two words, not necessarily adjacent, swap onset sounds (*brittle lick: little brick*), or syllables (*deckdot polkachair*). Visual nonsense is often achieved through unusual spelling patterns that sound correct but are misspelled (like Causley's *sphinx, thinx, blinx* rhymes).

● Allow children time to familiarise themselves with types of wordplay and misuse of syntax and experiment with silliness. Invite them to write a recipe poem, beginning *Take a handful of..../Add a pinch of...*
  ● Encourage them to invent nonsense words for the ingredients and, when this is secure, for the verbs (*Springle with melted flodge*).
  ● Demonstrate how easy it is to create rhymes with nonsense words. In fact, using nonsense words, you can even find words to rhyme with *borange* and *glurple*!

You Can... **Broaden the appeal of writing**

Poetry is arguably one of the hardest genres to 'write to order' and it is a huge expectation that we place on children to do so. On the other hand, there is virtually nothing that cannot become the subject of a poem, so the boundaries are limitless. Personal possessions, feelings and experience are perhaps the strongest triggers for any kind of poem, serious or light.

Thinking points

● When did you last try your hand at poetry writing? Put yourself in the child's shoes and have a go. Relax and go with the flow – who knows, the muse may be waiting to strike!

● As poems can be about anything, begin with the personal to lead to the universal. *My hand...* is so personally mine, yet everybody has one. So if I write about my hand, my readers can immediately relate to my poem. Thumbs up to hands – they touch everyone!

Tips, ideas and activities

● As a forerunner to writing, word-association games can free up and relax the mind to explore in broad directions. Try the clap-clap-clap speak-the-word game around the group without repeating any word. Point out to the children that the word can have a very loose or a close link with the previous word, but otherwise can be any associated word, even a rhyme is fine. (For example: house (clap-clap-clap) chimney (c-c-c) smoke (c-c-c) pipe (c-c-c) water (c-c-c) daughter...)

● A favourite object; anything the writer loves, could start a poem. Put its name at the centre of a spidergraph. Ask the children to jot down any smells, sounds or feelings associated with the object. Extend those personal and specific associations to broader links.

  ● So, for example, if they are writing about a toy pony – what do they know about real horses?
  ● If it's made of plastic, what spin-off associations does the material suggest?
  ● What about the word *horse*? – list word-rhymes: *course, force, gorse, Norse, sauce*; word-associations: *saddle, reins, ride, Ride a cock-horse, piebald, gallop, neigh* and so on.
  ● This collection of material forms a words-and-ideas-bank. Children can draw from this bank to create their poem.

● Share photocopiable page 60 as an example of how such a spidergraph of information can be turned into an imaginative poem. Point out how only selected ideas from the spidergraph appear in the final poem.

● Use an experience as a trigger for a light-hearted poem: A trip to... (the seaside; the shops; the cinema); My party; A bicycle ride. Ask the children to write a refrain or chorus to start them off before writing the verses in between. Remind them of the value of repetition.

You Can... Familiarise children with poetry forms

Sometimes the subject matter will suggest a structure for a poem. Sometimes a phrase or line will dictate a metre. The broader the range of poetry forms available to the children, the more confident the choices they make – so, like sewing with a wealth of embroidery stitches, they will build a richer picture.

Thinking points

● Display examples of different kinds of poetry in your classroom. Attach a brief description of the form as a quick reference.

● If children overuse rhyme – to the point of forcing rhyme to override meaning, ask them to attempt a syllable-counting form, such as haiku or cinquain. They do not preclude rhyme but make it less likely to creep in.

● Syllable-counting poems have cross-curricular advantages: they benefit phonic word-deciphering and spelling skills, as well as simple arithmetic.

Tips, ideas and activities

● Introduce children to the cinquain. Invented by the American poet Adelaide Crapsey, it has 5 lines: 22 syllables arranged in the sequence 2-4-6-8-2. This form of poem will lend itself to almost any subject matter. It can also form the pattern for a series of stanzas to make up a longer poem.

● Ask each child in the class for any two-syllabled word. Jot a list of around 30 on a board. Invite the children to choose a word as the first line of a cinquain. Use previously practised brainstorming techniques to stretch their imaginations while constraining ideas into 22 syllables. This is the perfect exercise for showing how hard every word in a poem has to work and how it must earn its right to be there! Unncessary, lightweight words will soon be kicked out.

● Give all the children the same subject matter and ask each child to write one cinquain on that theme. Join them all together for an extended joint poem. Invite other classes to join in – aim to create the longest poem in the school.

● Try a cinquain advert where the first line or the title is 'For sale'. For example:

FOR SALE
Used only once:
Bright pink polka-dot bike.
Will consider offers around
Five quid.

● In another session challenge the children to experiment with the same poem, retaining the basic ideas, but using a contrasting structure such as a rhyming couplet or a tongue-twister.

You Can... **Demonstrate the value of drafting and redrafting**

Trial and error and patient persistence pay dividends. You can demonstrate the basic principles of the drafting process in one session and have the children experiment for themselves. The real drafting process will happen over several sessions. Returning to work afresh another day often reveals clunky lines or weak words.

Thinking points

● A good poem makes the reader look at the world through the poet's eyes to see things anew.

● Use of imagery helps paint vivid pictures.

● The best possible words in the best possible order will not happen by accident. Lines will often need several revisions before they work well. Reassure the children that a thing worth doing is worth doing well.

Tips, ideas and activities

● Ask the children to imagine the sound of a plane flying overhead. Invite them to offer words to describe the noise, such as *moan* and *drone*. Look up suggestions in a thesaurus and add to the list: *hum, buzz, whine, grumble, complain*. Are these appropriate? (Bees usually buzz; people grumble and complain.) What if we personify the plane? Try: The plane grumbles across the sky. Continue to experiment together with different words. Is there a better preposition than *across*? Is there a more imaginative word than *sky*?

● Now challenge the children, in groups, to come up with the most polished original line they can think of. Limit them to five minutes before hearing and comparing the results. Point out how they have involved their senses and used imagery in the form of personification.

● Next, ask each group to personify the sky. How do the clouds feel about the plane? How do they behave? Do they float/scurry/sulk? Are there any vapour trails? Encourage children to use simile. What do the clouds look like?

● It's time to introduce another element to the poem. This might be someone on the ground looking up or another airborne creature flying much lower. Explain to the children that you want them to produce a thought-provoking poem that evokes atmosphere.

● As their poems progress, encourage the children to keep reading aloud. Two adjacent lines, however good individually, must also enhance each other. With practice, children will hear what sounds 'right' or 'better'. It will almost certainly include alliteration (repeated consonants) or assonance (repeated vowel sounds).

● Invite the children to experiment with changing the word order. For example, the first line might end up as (show the drafting process): ~~Across~~ *Through the* ~~sky~~ *pouting clouds* (personification + assonance) *a grumbling* (adjective from the verb *grumble*) *plane advances.*

You Can... **Provide a role model**

However confident you are at getting children to write poetry, there's nothing like inviting in a professional children's poet for the day. A performance will bring life to the printed word – as will a new voice and a fresh face. Children can ask questions on the writing process, enjoy a workshop and realise that writing is not just something teachers make you do. A visiting poet acts as an advocate for writing and a role model for the writer.

Thinking points

● If you plan to invite a poet into school discuss in advance what you want to come out of the day. Most writers are happy to tailor their input to suit your children's needs.

● Plan ahead – poets are often booked months in advance, especially for annual occasions like National Poetry Day (first Thursday in October) or World Book Day (March).

● Your poet may have travelled a long way to visit your school – make sure your welcome is warm!

● You will want as many children to benefit from your poet's visit as possible. Remember though, if you spread their time too thinly, the benefits will be superficial. Perhaps every child can hear a reading, reserving workshops (if offered) for one or two classes to delve deeper into the writing process.

● Timetable follow-up work to get full advantage from the experience.

Tips, ideas and activities

● Prepare your children for their visitor. What does a poet do? Do they know the poet's name? Look up the visitor in anthology indices and on the web so that children know who to expect and have some familiarity with their work.

● Consider if you would like your poet to stay after school and bring books along for signings and sale. Will you invite parents along after school? If your poet is travelling a long way, consider a two-day visit and perhaps schedule a teacher INSET. Some writers are happy to accept domestic hospitality or stay in an inexpensive B & B.

● If you plan to hot-seat your visitor, encourage the children to prepare some pertinent questions. Spontaneity is good too, but sometimes children need time to prepare – especially if they are shy.

● Be prepared to join in any writing exercises yourself. It's a great opportunity to experience how your children feel. It's also the perfect chance to observe children's reactions.

● Remember, poets are not teachers and should not be left in charge of the children. Classroom organisation and pupil control are up to you – though it is worth discussing how your visitor would like the children arranged. Also check when the poet would like questions to be asked and find out if they need any props.

● Many publishers have links with writers and will know who likes to work with which age-groups. They will be happy to put you in contact with poets who visit schools. It is also worth surfing the internet as many poets have their own websites. Sometimes funding help is available from local arts associations.

● The following websites are worth a visit. Poetry Zone also publishes children's poetry on its site.
  ● www.poetrysociety.org.uk
  ● www.poetryzone.co.uk
  ● www.classactagency.co.uk

You Can... **Enable children to appreciate each other's success**

The actual writing process is quite solitary and isolating. It is helpful for the children to hear how others got on. A plenary session goes some way to addressing this, but it doesn't allow time for great scope. If children put a lot of effort into their work it is greatly rewarding to be able to share and enjoy each other's success – especially, in the case of poetry, through readings and performance.

Thinking points

● Practice at voice projection is always useful before any reading – whether in class or in a hall.

● Standing up and facing the audience is important if others are to hear a child read. Preferably invite readers to the front of the class to avoid other children becoming restless if they can't hear.

● Allowing children to read in groups increases confidence, even if they read individually within the group.

● Try to arrange a safe plinth for the reader to stand on – it does not need to be very high, just enough to raise the reader's height and help a small voice to carry.

Tips, ideas and activities

● Children can be shy and diffident about reading their own words to others. Let them get used to reading favourite poems aloud from poetry anthologies first. Remind them to read more slowly than they would in their heads, to allow the audience to listen. (Listening to poems without the words in front of you takes practice, too.)

● Encourage the children to learn the words of a poem by heart so that they can look at their audience when they recite the poem.

● Provide opportunities for children to read their poems aloud (first to their own class, then to another class and then in assembly). Link poems together in a theme for a class assembly (such as 'caring for each other and the environment' or 'families').

● Create visual ways for children to share their poems with a wider audience. The school's newsletter, for example, could include a poetry page.

● Hold a vote for the favourite poem written by one of the children. Print the poems and give each child a sticky note to anonymously attach to the page of their favourite. Don't allow them to vote for their own! Display the winner's poem in pride of place.

● Create a Class Blog to show off the children's poems online and share them with a wider audience such as parents, governors and friends of the school.

● Look out for children's poetry competitions. The Poetry Society runs an annual competition for young writers. Other competitions also include a junior section – for example, the Ledbury Festival (Hereford) whose annual Under-11 three winning entrants receive book tokens. See www.poetry-festival.com.

● Make an audio tape of children reading their own poems. With accompanying printed text it makes a valuable classroom resource, highlighting both written and oral aspects of poetry.

You Can... Develop regular writing habits in children

School children will need to put pen to paper every day, but this is different from developing a writing habit. The need to write and the joy of writing are not necessarily the same thing. A writing habit renders writing as normal and everyday as speaking.

Thinking points

● Consider the many different functions and purposes of both speaking and writing. Which are necessary; which are not? The writing 'habit' goes beyond the necessary – it equates to the pleasurable daily conversation with friends rather than the functional asking for a day-return ticket or a granary loaf.

● You won't phone your friend in New Zealand every day, but you might write or email on a regular basis. Writing, although less frequent than speech, can be a regular aspect of everyday life.

● People don't (often!) talk to themselves, but they may keep a diary or journal; they may write reminder notes to themselves – even shopping lists. Putting things into words to ourselves helps us to assess and organise our own actions and lives.

Tips, ideas and activities

● All speech revolves around communication. Under this broad umbrella, ask the children to suggest imperatives for speaking. List their ideas, or offer examples from the following: Expressing requests, concern, approval, warning, explanation, feelings, reminders, invitations, answers or responses to others.

● Now ask them to think of occasions when they speak unnecessarily, although still, of course, for purposes of communication. List suggestions:
  ● greetings
  ● exchanging news and gossip with friends
  ● expressing opinions
  ● recommending something
  ● telling someone about aspects of your life.

● Explain that, just as the function of what we say varies (we have to ask the bus driver for a ticket; we don't have to tell our friend about our new fishing rod), so does what we write.

● Invite the children to choose a form of regular writing that they would like to try. This might be:
  ● A holiday or weekend journal (what they did, where they went and so on) for their own amusement and record.
  ● A daily diary (for their eyes only) recording what they did, what happened in the world and their feelings.
  ● A blog – similar to a diary, but inviting selected friends to read their news and feelings.
  ● Book reviews – a few lines about each book that they read; its title and author, year of publication, its basic plot, theme or subject matter; if and how they enjoyed it; its strengths and weaknesses.
  ● Letters to a relative or a pen-pal. This might be arranged with another school in a different part of the country. Set this up between like-minded children who are likely to stay the course. It can be frustrating if one of the writers fails to respond.

You Can... Demonstrate how good reading leads to better writing

In an age of sound-bites and channel-hopping it takes masterful writing to engage and retain a reader's attention. A 'good read' in terms of journalism is writing that will compete with other media and keep its fan-base and circulation figures. It will not necessarily be a faultless example of perfect use of the English language – but it will be easy to read and serve its purpose.

Thinking points

● Children will often have favourite comics and magazines, possibly relating to their interest areas. All reading is to be encouraged whether 'improving' or not!

● 'Meat and five veg a day' has its place in our diet, as does Shakespeare and *The Spectator*, but a bar of chocolate and *The Beano* are good too!

● Much of children's everyday reading will be in the past tense. Magazine articles give them experience of a mixture of tenses, especially the present.

Tips, ideas and activities

● Invite children to bring in a favourite magazine or comic, bookmarking an article or feature that they found interesting. Bring in some examples of your own, written at a child-friendly level.

● Invite the children, in pairs, to swap with each other, introducing their article and explaining why they found it entertaining and/or informative. After reading each other's choices, ask the children to discuss any areas of agreement or disagreement in terms of interest level, style of writing and presentation, making notes about their own chosen article in the process. For example:

- Text in coloured boxes made points stand out.
- Short sentences made it easy to read.
- Captions to pictures linked content with illustration.
- Quotations from the main body of text, as subheadings within the text, encouraged me to dip in to find out more.
- It didn't seem very informative, and told the reader the same thing but in different ways.
- I'd like to have read about an aspect of the text in greater depth and detail.
- The proportion of text to illustration was too high.

● Drawing on their findings, ask the children to write a magazine article based on the style of their choice. They should adapt their content according to their findings, but aim at the same readership. Their subject matter may differ but should be in keeping with the magazine's target market. Ask them to imagine they are writing for the editor of their publication. How can they match the style, length and content of the published article?

● Encourage children to develop their writing into a simulated magazine page (using a desktop publishing program if possible). Put the articles in a loose-leaf file for everyone to enjoy. Hold a vote for 'Journalist of the Week'.

You Can... **Help children to write with authority**

The written word lasts longer than the spoken word. It can be read and re-read, analysed, discussed and picked apart. Putting something in writing holds connotations over and above word of mouth, hence written contracts; written quotations for commissioned work; written laws, agreements and reports. Words that are going to have impact must be chosen carefully and must be accurate and unambiguous.

Thinking points

● Background knowledge and factual support adds authority to what would otherwise be the simple expression of opinions.

● Short sentences are less likely to lead to ambiguity than longer ones.

● Using too much jargon may lead to poor understanding.

● Reading aloud helps to show up any inconsistencies, irrelevancies or poor continuity.

● Adding detailed factual information to a bald statement adds authority and conviction and sounds more compelling.

Tips, ideas and activities

● Ask the children to write a list of ten things they know as facts. These could be personal or universal. (*My name is...*; *The sun rises in the east and sets in the west.*)

● Now ask them to write a list of ten things that they believe or think but cannot prove as a fact, such as *Fairies live in the woods.*

● Ask individuals to read aloud one of their statements, from the 'I know' list and add a sentence or two to support their fact. For instance, *I know the sun rises in the east and sets in the west, because I watched it rise this morning. In fact, the sun does not so much rise, as we turn towards it as our planet rotates over the twenty-four hours that form a day and a night.*

● Invite others to choose from their 'I believe/think' list, adding support of pseudo 'facts'. Such as, *I know there are fairies in the woods because there are hollows in the toadstools where the fairies have sat in them.*

● If children use the words *I think* or *I believe*, ask them to repeat their statement omitting these modifying words. Similarly, point out how such phrases as *sort of* diminish the strength of their argument.

● Finally, ask each child to choose one of their statements, known or believed, and write a persuasive piece of writing, developing their theme and adding information. Ask them to write it as a speech to create impact and impress their audience. Explain that positive statements carry more weight than negative ones.

● Remind children to support what they say with examples and evidence (even in 'I think' examples, such as researching the names of concave-headed toadstools!).

You Can... Initiate the use of effective writing aids

All publications have their own house style, including newspapers and magazines. It is recognisable in their format and style of language; their way of wording information. It means that any page the reader looks at will have a degree of uniformity about it. Reading will be easy in terms of vocabulary and sentence construction. Reporters tend to use no unnecessary words.

Thinking points

● When thinking of writers' aids, dictionaries and thesauri come to mind. Everyday 'copy' writers, such as newspaper reporters, are more likely to turn to their house style guide as their first point of reference.

● Have you ever heard someone begin to speak and got an instant sinking feeling? It is born of the immediate knowledge that they will use a lot of words and say very little – 'In my particular sphere of operations…' one man began; 'At work…', I substituted, silently! Effective writing does not mean more words.

● We live in an age of jargon. It is possible to convey meaning without it!

Tips, ideas and activities

● Bring in a few different editions of the same magazine or newspaper. Ask the children to scan the text to look for similar pieces of information. For example, examine how the people making the news have their names featured (full names or initials?); the sort of speech marks used for direct quotations and whether the reporting style is consistent throughout the publication (compare front page news items; page 5 news items; back page sports reports).

● Explain that the conventions adopted by a newspaper or magazine are called the 'house style'. Journalists and reporters are expected to stick to the house rules in the way they present their 'copy' – the name given to the articles they write.

● Hand out a copy of photocopiable page 61 to each group of three to four children. These are incomplete 'house style' sheets for an imaginary newspaper. Invite the children to examine copies of newspapers to discern further style rules to add to the sheet. Suggest the following areas:
  ● How many words are in the average sentence?
  ● How are sports results presented?
  ● What kind of words may be left out of headlines?
  ● Which punctuation marks are most commonly used?
  ● Are there many adjectives used?
    ● Do news reports of events offer any opinions or simply facts?
    ● Do sentences follow on logically from one to the next?

● Help the children to turn what they have discovered into a rule, such as, 'Stick to facts'.

● In writing descriptive prose, the children will be used to looking for longer words and evocative expressions. When writing reports these are to be avoided. Help the children to recognise this by doing a verb-search through a newspaper finding the simplest verbs they can, such as *went*, *stayed* and *died*, rather than *proceeded*, *remained* and *passed away*.

You Can... **Help children check for accuracy and clarity**

When all else fails, read the instructions! Whether it's an adult trying to assemble a piece of flat-pack furniture, or a child with a new game, we're all guilty of reading the instructions as a last resort. Our reluctance to 'read the rules' is possibly our impatience to 'get on with the game', but it may be that we suspect the instructions will be wordy, obscure and, basically, less than helpful. Often, we are right!

Thinking points

- Readers are human. Humans are lazy. Instructions should be as clear and concise as possible – and numbering helps!

- If we hear a new joke the first thing we want to do is try it out on someone else. Will they react as we did and laugh (or groan)? But we often hear someone ruin the telling of a good joke by leaving out an essential element until too late or giving away the ending through poor telling!

- Instructions exemplify the importance of order, accuracy and clarity. It is better to have 'Pre-heat the oven' as the first instruction, than read 'Put it in a pre-heated oven' as the final instruction after half-an-hour's preparation.

- Reading all the instructions to the end *before* beginning a task, rather than one at a time, is a good habit to adopt!

Tips, ideas and activities

- Invite the children to plan instructions to teach somebody how to perform a task, play a game or make something. In the planning process, allow them to perform the task themselves, making notes as they do so. Examples of activities include: a ball or board game of their own invention; a gymnastic or dance routine; how to play a recorder; how to draw a horse.

- When the children have finished note-making, ask them to make a fair copy of their instructions. They must avoid diagrams or illustrations and rely on the written word. Give advice on use of textual devices, such as tips (in boxes or highlighted); numbered instructions; warnings and expectations along the way. Encourage the children to use positive imperatives rather than negative, such as *Grip the paper at one corner* rather than *Don't hold the edge of the paper.*

- Ask the children to find a partner who does not know anything about their activity to test out their instructions.

- If there is difficulty in understanding a given instruction, children who are testing 'the rules' should first ask another child if they can interpret the text before returning to the author for clarification. Authors should note any clunky wording, missing instructions and so on.

- In a plenary session, invite the children to evaluate each other's work. Remind them that they are assessing the efficacy of the instructions, not the activity itself. They might do this by giving marks out of five under various headings or by way of a feedback tick-form with five rows:

	Excellent	Very good	Good	Poor	Very poor
Clarity					
Completeness					
Reading ease					
Accuracy					
Conciseness					

You Can... **Open children's eyes to the power of writing**

When we hear someone give a great speech we have to remember that someone – either the orator or someone with shared conviction – wrote the words. The timing of the speech, its physical and historical setting, and its manner of delivery will all influence public reaction. But without memorable words it would fall flat. Words are powerful tools.

Thinking points

● Consider what makes a great speech: words that stir us to respond in agreement; words used emotively to achieve that reaction in the listener; words used to make us consider a new idea or perspective.

● Keep in mind the value of debate. Knowing how to present a case, evaluate others' arguments and express our own is a gift for life.

● Consider the etiquette of speech making. Speeches are intended to be listened to without interruption. Heckling is the name given to rude and noisy interruptions to someone's speech.

● Writing and speaking are closely related. Get the first right and the second will follow.

Tips, ideas and activities

● Encourage children to research famous speeches – the powerful words of Elizabeth I during the Spanish Armada (*I know I have but the body of a weak and feeble woman; but I have the heart and stomach of a king*); Jesus' sermon on the mount (*Blessed are the meek: for they shall inherit the Earth*); Martin Luther King's visionary words (*I have a dream...*). Look at these websites:
  ● www.famousquotes.me.uk/speeches
  ● www.americanrhetoric.com/speeches

● Ask the children to plan a speech on some aspect of life about which they feel strongly. It doesn't have to be about a life-changing subject – can be anything from a speech to congratulate their grandmother on her birthday or a speech to parents on why a pet would be a good idea! The aim is to convince their audience that what they say is right, indisputable, and considered.

● Suggest to children that they may use visual aids to support their speech such as a banner or placard or a bullet-pointed list to sum up points made at the end.

● Remind them that a speech involves introducing the subject matter, speaking and then summing up!

● When the children have drafted their speeches, ask them to practise them aloud to look for ways to improve and strengthen them. List the following points for children to check against their writing:
  ● Opening line – does it grab listeners' attention?
  ● Content – is it straightforward and direct?
  ● Pace – avoid lingering too long on one aspect or unnecessary detail.
  ● Flow – do points lead and follow logically?
  ● Length – will it hold the listeners' attention?
  ● Overuse of phraseology – avoid using similar words or expressions too often or too close together.

You Can... Motivate children to write for pleasure

Children who enjoy creative writing may find the prospect of writing a non-fiction piece off-putting. However, the best non-fiction should be as readable as fictional narrative. Facts and non-chronological reports do not need to be dry in their presentation. Look for examples of exciting writing to use as models for the children's writing. The conversational style of David Attenborough's nature writing is a prime example of how the author can involve the reader, as if in enthusiastic conversation with a friend.

Thinking points

● Rhetorical questions in place of statements involve the reader and bring variety into a text.

● Interspersing anecdotes, especially based on personal experience, helps prevent non-fiction writing from becoming dry and boring.

● Labelled diagrams break up a text visually as well as supporting the text.

● A non-fiction writer must make the reader enthusiastic about the subject matter. It is worth examining how authors do this and, equally, how and why some succeed better than others.

● Consider how good non-fiction writers make their writing accessible to everyone, rather than just a few specialists in the subject.

Tips, ideas and activities

● List the following examples of non-fiction paragraph starters. All address and involve the reader directly, as if in conversation. They serve to challenge the reader to read on; to stimulate and interest the reader's mind; to invite a questioning mind.

  ● Have you ever wondered how...?
  ● Anyone can find out about... all you need is...
  ● Did you know that...?
  ● Let's go back to a time when...
  ● How would you feel if...?
  ● You might think that... but...
  ● Where would you go to find...?

● Point out that every paragraph will not use such attention-grabbing techniques. These will be broken up by more factual paragraph openings such as: *A hundred years ago...* or *There are 300 different species of... .*

● Ask the children to choose a subject of interest to themselves or a topic subject that they are studying. Invite them to list ten bare facts on the subject; some general and some specific. Challenge the children to expand each of these facts into paragraphs. Some may be combined within a paragraph; others may provide enough content and information to occupy a whole paragraph. As they write, ask the children to find ways to involve the reader, using the listed examples as models. Remind them that, over the whole piece of writing, it is not necessary for every opening to be of the 'direct address' nature.

● Encourage children to develop the layout of their non-fiction in a reader-friendly format. Ask what they could add to enhance it, such as an inset box of 'Fun Facts' that highlight or complement aspects of the main body of writing, or a mini-quiz at the close of their report.

You Can... Demonstrate how writing can empower children

Human beings are a contrary lot: half the time we want to preserve the comfortably familiar status quo and the other half of the time we want to see changes made! We can debate a point; we can fight our corner; we can hold enquires. Ultimately, if we want to achieve the desired change (or preservation) it will most likely involve writing a report.

Thinking points

● Facts carry more weight than conjecture. Teach children where to look for support for their evaluations of situations.

● Red herrings and woolly thinking often distract from valid argument. Teach children how to stick to the point. Reading aloud will often clarify thinking and show us where there are errors, repetitions or omissions.

● Support for an argument can come from the results of others' fact-finding missions or from like-minded individuals or organisations. If you want to help in saving the whale, it's better to approach the Whale and Dolphin Conservation Society than the Norwegian or Japanese fishing industrialists!

Tips, ideas and activities

● Children will be familiar with the concept of reports. As the time for their school report approaches you may see them watching their manners, their behaviour and their work performance. Why? They want a 'good report'. Discuss what constitutes a 'good report'. Is it just saying nice things? Is it uncritical acclaim for someone or something? Or does it assess by measurable means, such as test results, quantifiable levels of improvement, actual visible data?

● Discuss with the children how parliament and councils operate when making decisions. They may have fact-finding missions and public enquiries, and they may assess statistical evidence, but, ultimately, there will be a written report.

● Divide the class into groups of six. Ask them to discuss something they would like to see changed. Tell them to plan a report on the issue. For example, suppose they wanted the playground to be more child-friendly. Are there seats or benches in a quiet area? Is there shade against the hot sun? Is there a climbing frame or goal? Are the infants separated from the more boisterous juniors and their footballs?

● Suggest that each group acts like a committee, allocating areas of research and paragraphs of the report. Remind the children, when writing their reports, to attribute any statistics or quoted facts to their source. Ideas include:
  ● An interview with the headteacher; an infant; a junior.
  ● An opinion poll across the class, school or year-group.
  ● A statistical report – how many injuries result from one child running into another?
  ● Wider research – the dangers of exposure to the sun and the need for children to exercise aerobically.

● Ask the children to revise their writing, making sure that they are using only factual phraseology rather than assumptions, speculation or unattributed opinion.

You Can... **Enable children to match style with purpose**

We naturally adopt different styles of speech and levels of formality when talking to different people. In the space of an hour we may chat to a friend, exchange information with a colleague, discuss formal arrangements with a service provider and report to a senior. In speech, we naturally adapt our form of language, our choice and delivery of words, as a matter of course. Different styles of writing are an extension of this modification of speech.

Thinking points

● Reading from a variety of sources also helps the reader to recognise different styles and adapt their own writing accordingly. By selecting favourite books within a genre the children are making choices about their preferred styles of writing.

● Reading aloud is the quickest way of assessing the written word. This way we soon develop an 'ear' for what sounds 'right'.

● Children are often good mimics. Exploit their talents by letting them demonstrate talking in the style of a familiar TV soap or children's character – as well as being entertaining, it highlights different uses of language!

Tips, ideas and activities

● Encourage the children to role-play different situations and characters, formal and informal, improvising speech and adapting vocabulary and delivery accordingly. Invite the rest of the group to comment on how and why speech patterns change. For example, ask groups of three children to act out the following scenarios, or similar:

  ● Mother telling off child for untidy bedroom; 'posh' neighbour rings doorbell and mother's speech-style changes both to neighbour and to child. How does the vocabulary change?

  ● Child being interviewed by newsagent for a paper-round. Child is not offered job, as too young. Child then relates the event to a peer. How will these conversations differ?

  ● Man trying to sell a car to a stranger who decides not to buy. Friend of car salesman then comes along and asks about the car. How does the owner's style of speech alter?

● Explain how writing, like speech, varies according to purpose. Hand out copies of photocopiable page 62. Ask the children to read the extracts with a partner and discuss the different genres. This will help the children to define how language is used – ask them to compare the chatty tone of the letter with the narrative tone of the story extract. Tell the children that a successfully written informal letter should be written as if speaking to the reader face to face.

● Invite the children to take one of the extracts and rewrite it in another genre – for example, rewrite the story extract as a diary entry or the poem as a description in prose, and so on.

● Ask the children to write in a specific genre (as required), using the activity sheet as a reminder, together with further examples of the specified style.

You Can... Develop listening skills to improve writing and vice versa

Sometimes we write to help us listen. At other times we listen to help us write. Listening and writing co-exist in our lives on a daily basis. It may be noting a telephone message; it may be listening to the multiple choices to know which number to press when calling some service. Or it may simply be listening to what somebody says, face to face, and making notes before we forget. The better we listen, the easier and more accurate our writing.

Thinking points

● Quite often we listen selectively. Sometimes this is fine; at other times we need to listen in a more sustained way. Taking notes can aid concentration and confirm understanding. It provides a real and useful purpose for writing.

● Evidence suggests that our visual memory makes most of us poor eye-witnesses. Consider how note-making can improve our powers of observation and encourage a multi-sensory approach to developing memory.

● Lined paper tends to invite formality and may inhibit the ability to jot down notes. Try providing plain paper for note-making.

Tips, ideas and activities

● Invite parents, perhaps once a month, to come in and talk about their job, a hobby or a sport that would interest the children: a fire-fighter, a taxi driver, a police-officer, a horse-rider, a midwife, the lollipop patroller, a parent with a newborn baby. Ask the visitor to prepare a short talk for the children. Arm the class with clipboards and writing materials. Invite questions at the end of the talk and encourage the children to take notes.

● Take notes yourself to demonstrate how this does not mean 'head-down constant scribbling' every time the speaker speaks! Show how single words can be expanded into sentences later. An adequate level of note-making could be, for example, *litter – 6 – eyes open 3 weeks*.

● Schools can, and often do, create the opportunity for older, reliable children to practise their listening and note-making skills. They allow them to answer the phone during the staff's lunch-break. It is nicer for callers to speak to a human being than a machine and gives children a sense of responsibility. As a caller, I always think it reflects well on the school.

● Encourage children to make notes as they listen to audio reports or stories. Ask them to write a résumé or a retelling of the story from their notes.

● When setting children a task, occasionally invite them to take notes as you dictate what you want them to do and in what order. Keep slower writers together so that you can repeat instructions quietly, as necessary, without disturbing more fluent writers.

● Hold a class discussion about an issue and afterwards ask the children to present the main points made in favour or against the point of discussion.

You Can... Use children's sense of community to improve writing skills

A school is often the hub of the community, bringing together people from many different walks of life with family and other interests in common. Local events, school activities and fundraising events all bring the community together. These are great opportunities for the children to get involved in many different ways, using a variety of skills.

Thinking points

● Linking learning activities with events beyond the classroom walls gives children extra motivation and a real purpose and showcase for their work.

● Children delight in seeing their posters displayed in the windows of public buildings (where they are unlikely to be vandalised).

● Seeking co-operation from other local organisations, such as the library, helps to strengthen links between the school and the wider community.

● Encourage teamwork – children's computer design, desktop publishing and word-processing skills can complement the longhand writers' creative skills.

Tips, ideas and activities

● Whatever the planned event, your class can provide the written work to support it. Ideas include:
  ● posters and flyers to advertise the event
  ● circulars to take home
  ● a letter inviting a local celebrity to open the event
  ● a letter or advertisement in the local newspaper
  ● bookmarks promoting the cause.

● Discuss how the wording in each of these will differ. Who are they aimed at? What do the recipients need to know in advance? For example, a circular to parents might include a request for offers of help on the day and so on. By contrast, a flyer to be distributed further afield, might simply give information such as date, time, venue and the main attractions.

● Help children to match their writing to its purpose. Ask them to notice when travelling by car or bus how many words they have time to read as they pass road signs, words in shop windows, notices and commercial posters. What features make them take notice of the material? Discuss issues of presentation and content: size of print, colour and arrangement of text, short statements, attention-grabbing slogans, few full sentences.

● After the children have drafted the content, they will need to structure the text – deciding what is essential and how, and in what order, it should appear. This, of itself, forces revision as well as the checking of spelling and grammar.

● Encourage the children to emulate the text of signs and advertisements around them – use of the imperative tense, snappy slogans and arresting words.

● After the event children can write:
  ● a report for parents or the school newsletter
  ● thank-you letters to those outside the school who helped.

You Can... **Enable children to organise their thoughts**

Have you ever made any new year resolutions – the kind you really intended to keep? Did you feel more likely to stick to them if you wrote them down? Somehow, the act of writing down thoughts, opinions and intentions gives them gravity and permanence. Which is probably why, when we say, 'I'm going to clean the windows every Sunday without fail,' those who know us best will ask, 'Can I have that in writing?'!

Thinking points

● If we write down our thoughts or intentions it may go some way to making a contract with ourselves, but mainly, it helps us to organise our thoughts and check that they make sense.

● When we write about something after the event, a journal entry, a letter home, a book or film review, we are also setting out our feelings and reactions in a more formal presentation than simple thoughts. We are telling ourselves, this is how it was; this is how I felt; this is what happened.

● Sometimes when we appear to be writing for someone else's benefit, it may well be that, at least in part, we are reassessing our own lives, the world in general, and our own role and relationship to it. (Perhaps that is what annual, seasonal round-robin letters to family and friends are all about!)

Tips, ideas and activities

● Ask the children's opinion about a recent event or experience, such as the latest class assembly, the most recently read book, the latest film at the cinema and so on. Encourage the children to make brief comments and reactions before asking others for their opinions. Do they agree or disagree? Invite the children to highlight areas that have not been mentioned. For example, of a film, perhaps setting, casting and costume, rather than simply plot and action.

● Tell the children that you would like them to tackle a piece of writing: a review of something they have seen or done, or somewhere they have visited. Ask them to use paragraphs to organise their thoughts into different aspects of the experience. Explain how the opening paragraph will be a general introduction; middle paragraphs will break up their thoughts according to which aspect they are recording; saving the final paragraph for summing up and drawing a conclusion.

● In a separate session, ask the children to tackle a piece of writing that looks ahead – a plan of action. This could be, say, preparations for a party – who to invite; what to wear; where to hold it (venue); any special theme (fancy dress, magic); what food and drink to provide; music; entertainment; decorations and so on. Discuss how this piece of writing will differ from the retrospective piece. Will they need paragraphs? Full sentences? What about other organisational devices such as bullet points, numbering, boxes for special attention (such as *Phone conjuror: Tuesday*).

● If it's the appropriate time of year, challenge your children to write their new year resolutions. Alternatively, next week's resolutions or 'How I plan to turn over a new leaf'.

You Can... Encourage children to use ICT effectively

What did we do before computers? Well, I am old enough to remember using tracing paper for maps and carbon paper for extra copies – and reach for heavy volumes of encyclopedias. Now I find myself clicking on the PC thesaurus rather than reaching for a book – a dangerously limiting habit! Reference resources are plentiful on the world wide web, as are downloadable maps, pictures and texts. Using these judiciously can be an asset to writing.

Thinking points

● An increasing number of books that are out of copyright are available in full on the world wide web, including the complete works of Shakespeare.

● Before downloading text or illustrations, make sure that no-one is infringing copyright. Most sites include information on what does and does not. Personal use is normally not a problem. Displaying material on an interactive whiteboard can carry a different status.

● ICT is just one resource. It should be a tool not a dictator. Never neglect or underestimate the value of first-hand experience and old-fashioned books.

● It is prudent to teach children to be sceptical of all sources. Never rely on one source of information as wholly reliable, whether in print on paper or in digital form on a website.

Tips, ideas and activities

● Artistic children will always enjoy illustrating their work; children who can't draw will not! Encourage children to search for clip art to enhance the presentation of their work. This is especially useful if children are producing a leaflet, giving a presentation or printing a flyer or class newspaper. Alternatively, for children who do like drawing, digital photographs or scanned copies of their drawings can appear within text, reduced to an appropriate size. Reducing the scale has the added advantage of diminishing any 'dodgy' draughtsmanship, so children will often be more delighted with their printed illustrations than they were with their original pencil work!

● For full online texts of classic literature, such as *The Wizard of Oz* or *The Water Babies*, take a look a: www.literature.org and www.bibliomania.com. These sites are useful for your own research and lesson preparation, as well as for the children's use directly. Even if you want your class to read an extract from a concrete copy of the original book, it is a helpful resource to use alongside the book. For example, with an electronic version of the text your browser can search to pinpoint a particular scene or linguistic example – easier than looking through the book at length, armed only with the knowledge that what you're looking for comes 'somewhere towards the end of the book'!

● Traditional encyclopaedias are a great resource for general research but, for up-to-date information and news, encourage children to investigate the news website www.thenewspaper.org.uk. It is aimed at children while also demonstrating a journalistic style of writing and presentation. Again, remind children that this is only one source of information and it is always wise to find a second or third source for confirmation rather than taking anything read at face value.

You Can... **Enrich and broaden children's active vocabulary**

Have you ever studied a foreign language and then tested it abroad? The foreign visitor always ends up understanding more than they can speak. It's easier to interpret words we hear, or gather the gist of meaning, than to come up with the words in the first place. It is the same for children – and indeed adults – in their first language: the passive vocabulary is always greater than the active vocabulary.

Thinking points

● In the conversations of daily life, most of us get by on a few hundred words. No wonder our active vocabulary is so much smaller than our passive vocabulary!

● Broadening and enriching vocabulary does not mean arbitrarily replacing single-syllabled words with multi-syllabled – *start* is usually preferable to *commencement*! On the other hand, we may fly – but our plane may soar!

● It is fun and necessary to try to work out the meaning of words from context, but equally important to be aware of the dangers of guessing without checking. It is easy to think we know what a word means and be mistaken.

Tips, ideas and activities

● Your children may be used to keeping a word-log of new words and their meanings, but how willing and confident are they to use those words in their own speaking and writing? Try issuing a challenge to your class to use each new word that they log within the week. Suggest that, as well as defining the word, they create a memorable sentence to keep it in. To this day, I still remember my first encounter with the lovely word *ephemeral* – it rolled off the tongue and I longed to use it, but feared the 'Have you swallowed a dictionary?' accusation. If all the class are competing to use new words, noone will look askance, and using useful and interesting words becomes 'the norm'.

● When using shared texts, keep a class log of new or interesting words. Create opportunities to use these new words in as many different contexts as possible. Make it a feature of your class that everyone seizes the opportunity to use the new words correctly. Keep a scoring system for each use and see which new word 'wins' the most uses by the end of the week or the month.

● Occasionally listing more unusual words (such as *predatory*, *intrepid* and *mugwump*) for children to look up provides good practice for dictionary work while increasing the children's vocabulary.

● Encourage the children to note the derivation and etymology of new words and learn more words in the process. Alternatively, offer related words for the children to identify the root of and guess at the meaning before looking it up. For example, if *amicable* means 'friendly', what do *amiable* and *amorous* mean?

● Suggest that children add glossaries to their non-fiction writing as and when appropriate, such as in specific topic work.

Scribble and scrawl

Scribble and Scrawl by Celia Warren

Scrawl and scribble, scribble and scrawl:
I cannot read these words at all.
Some letters are big and some are small
And one word looks about to fall.
Some lean forward, some lean back,
Some letters set off on a different track.
A few words look as if they're fighting...
But now what I wrote comes flooding back:
Remember to practise your handwriting.

Scrawl and scribble, scribble and scrawl:

I cannot read these words at all.

Some letters are big and some are small

And one word looks about to fall.

Some lean forward and some lean back,

Some letters set off on a different track.

A few words look as if they're fighting...

But now what I wrote comes flooding back:

Remember to practise your handwriting

Paraphrase without plagiarism

- Read the non-fiction text in the box below.
- Note how the first paragraph has been annotated and highlighted.
- Read the rewrite at the foot of the page, reworded by the annotator.
- Continue marking the rest of the text to show up the main points and key words.
- Draw on this and other sources to write your own information text.

Key words:
Wolves live
6–8 years

Main points underlined

→ habitat

→ of territory

THE GREY WOLF (Latin name: canus lupus) By Celia Warren

Prowling in the <u>tundra and forests of North America</u> are packs of grey wolves. Wolves, as wild as the wilderness they inhabit, can live to be twenty, but around six to eight years is more common. The grey wolf is extremely <u>territorial</u>, its home range <u>rarely overlapping</u> that of another pack, unless food is scarce. All members of <u>a pack will help patrol and defend their territory, of eight square miles to five thousand square miles</u>. Its size will depend on availability of prey.

The wolf's keen sense of smell helps it to find food. Its prey, usually larger than itself, include deer, bison and mountain sheep. As each wolf needs around a kilo of food per day, wolves also snack on smaller prey such as fish, rabbits and small rodents. Hunting in packs, of anything from two to twelve related wolves, and running at speeds of 30 miles per hour, they can cover large distances in their pursuit of prey.

It is easy to spot the leader of the pack, the alpha male. He will show his dominance by baring his teeth in a snarl of authority over the others. The hair on his back will rise and his ears will point forwards, sharp and alert. Only the leader of the pack will mate, but when he does, it will be for life. Females give birth to around seven pups per litter in underground dens. After two months the pups are weaned from their mothers' milk. Then, the adults regurgitate food for the pups to eat until they are big enough to hunt for themselves.

Wolves communicate through diverse yelps and calls. They growl, snarl and often howl. Howling helps members of a pack to locate and alert each other to the exciting presence of a deer, for example. Not all their communication is vocal; the tail position and their bodily pose can also express emotions to other wolves. Their body scent, too, gives out warnings, not least marking their territory to warn off other packs.

Opening of a new article drawing on information from the text above

Wolves live in the arctic regions of North America. For all six to eight years of their lives, they hunt in packs of up to a dozen, strongly defending their territory against neighbouring packs. Pack territory can cover as little as eight square miles or up to a vast five thousand mile area. It all depends on the density of deer, bison and other prey available for them to hunt.

Name: _____ Date: _____

Writing assessment

Tick box	Title of writing:	My tick box	My teacher's tick box
I aim to	targets	**I can**	**You did**
	use capital letters and full stops		
	use connectives to join simple sentences		
	use a range of punctuation		
	divide my writing into paragraphs		
	use tense consistently		
	use pronouns consistently		
	use interesting adjectives		
	use strong verbs		
	keep my writing a consistent size and spacing		

I can ....

I am pleased with ....

I could have done better by ....

Signed (my name) ....

You can ....

I am pleased with ....

You could have done better by ....

Signed (my teacher's name) ....

Storyboarding and plotting

Timeline:

Character: ambition ⟶ main obstacle ⟶

....

overcome how? ⟶ next problem ⟶ solution?

⟶ ambition achieved?/outcome?

....

Storyboarding: the main series of events as snapshots of the plot:

1	2
3	4
5	6

Broaden the appeal of writing

A wooden ornamental dog was the inspiration for the poem below.
Look at this spidergraph. It began with the word 'dog' in the
middle. Then the poet brainstormed related words and ideas.
Only the ideas underlined ended up in the finished poem.

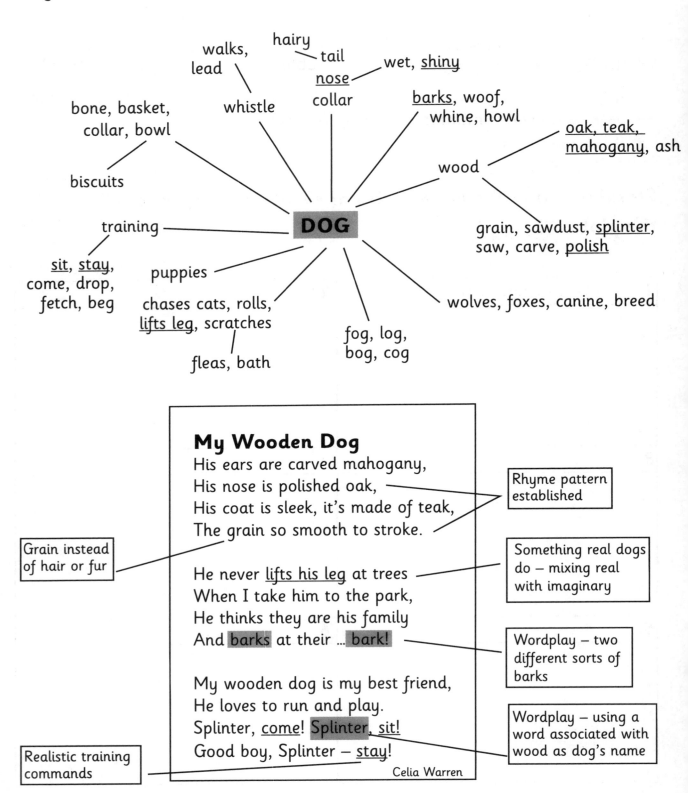

My Wooden Dog
His ears are carved mahogany,
His nose is polished oak,
His coat is sleek, it's made of teak,
The grain so smooth to stroke.

He never lifts his leg at trees
When I take him to the park,
He thinks they are his family
And barks at their ... bark!

My wooden dog is my best friend,
He loves to run and play.
Splinter, come! Splinter, sit!
Good boy, Splinter – stay!

Celia Warren

Rhyme pattern
established

Something real dogs
do – mixing real
with imaginary

Wordplay – two
different sorts of
barks

Wordplay – using a
word associated with
wood as dog's name

Grain instead
of hair or fur

Realistic training
commands

The Daily Scoop house style sheet

Rules for reporters writing for *The Daily Scoop*
These rules help all our reporters to adopt a similar writing style.

1. Never use capital letters unless you have to, for example, names of people or places: *Mr Blake, Councillor Penny Swan, Florin Avenue*.
2. If you are writing about committees, do not use capitals, for example, *the parks and woods committee*.
3. If you are shortening the name of a society or club, such as *the Florin Avenue Flower Arrangers' Society*, write the name in full the first time you use it, with its initials in brackets. Use the abbreviation thereafter (*FAFAS*).
4. You can use well-known abbreviations, such as *MP* (Member of Parliament), without explanation.
5. If writing numbers, use the full written word (*one, two, six...*) up to ten. For numbers beyond ten, use numerals instead (*11, 2000, 142*).

6. ....

....

7. ....

....

8. ....

....

9. ....

....

10. ....

Match style and purpose

- Here are extracts from different sources.
- In what sort of publication do you think each appeared?
- Choose from the list below and, briefly, explain your choice.

Anthology	Diary	Instruction manual	Newspaper
Atlas	Dictionary	Letter	Novel
Autobiography	Encyclopedia	Magazine	Recipe book

Tyger! Tyger! burning bright In the forests of the night, What immortal hand or eye Could frame thy fearful symmetry? In what distant deeps or skies Burnt the fire of thine eyes? On what wings dare he aspire? What the hand dare seize the fire?	Spinton's football season gets off to a flying start this weekend. Fans are eager to watch new captain, Josh Spink, take them to the top of the league. A tough tackler and brilliant scorer (25 goals last season), Spink is renowned for his skilful penalty shots and his inspiring energy.
The children stepped suddenly into a pool of sunlight. They had reached a clearing in the forest. For a while, neither spoke. Sally blinked and squinted. Joe brushed away a fly. Was this the place Old Kob had told them about? Joe opened his mouth to speak but stopped as his sister grabbed his arm, her finger to her lips. Someone, or something, was moving through the bracken only yards from where they stood.	Went to Butterfly & Otter Farm. Saw otters being fed. The keeper threw meat & fish for them to eat. He said one bit him last week! Shopping later – bought key ring & T-shirt. Bumped into Daz – arranged to meet 2moro. Ate at burger place. Swimming in evg. Watched DVDs till v v v late!
Melt butter in hot pan. Add flour slowly, stirring constantly, until mixture is the texture of breadcrumbs. Add milk gradually, stirring all the time. Do not allow to boil. Stir in grated cheese until melted.	We expect to arrive in town around lunchtime. Do you have any suggestions of the best place to meet? Very much looking forward to seeing you again after so long. You probably won't recognise me as I've grown my hair. Will you be bringing your dog? Give him a pat from me and tell him I've forgiven him for the mud-shower he gave me during our walk by the canal.

Index

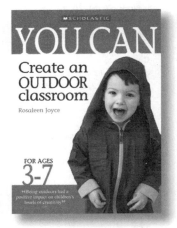

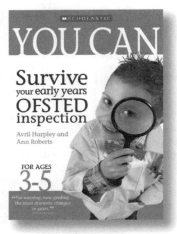